Psychologist Shawn Smith offer advice about evaluating a man partner.  *The Practical Guide to Men* addresses the traits a stable man exhibits, and the warning signs you would be wise to look for when you are evaluating whether a man is the right one for you. If you are trying to decide whether a man you're dating could be the one you give your heart to, you will want to read this book.

—**Neil Rosenthal,** syndicated relationship advice columnist and author of *Love, Sex, and Staying Warm*

The Practical Guide to Men is a must-have for any woman confused about finding the man of her dreams—or deciding whether she has already found him. Dr. Smith's conversational style is easy to read while also offering useful insights. He clarifies the complicated and often confusing world of men as potential partners. If you are wondering how to find a good man, or whether a particular man is worth keeping, this is the book for you!

—**Leslie Becker-Phelps, PhD,** author of *Insecure in Love*

Filled with wisdom, this book not only gives practical advice about looking outward for a life partner, but recognizes that the real works starts within. True and instantly useful, this is a very important book for men and women alike.

—**Linda Carroll,** author of *Love Cycles*

Women make mistakes far too often in their choice of men. *The Practical Guide to Men* explains why, and it offers practical strategies for avoiding common mistakes. You will find information that will help keep your eyes wide open when it really counts. The book is an engaging and eye-opening read, guaranteed to be useful for any woman seeking a dream companion for life.

—**Susan Page,** author of *If I'm So Wonderful, Why Am I Still Single?*

Shawn Smith has done it again with his latest book! With a deft hand at applying research, humor, and clinical savvy to common relationship question, *The Practical Guide to Men* is a wise and fascinating look at how to recognize a truly good man. Women will benefit from this brilliant insider's view into the male psyche, while men will find help refining their relationship readiness. A spectacular read.

—**Shannon Kolakowski, PsyD,** author of *Single, Shy, and Looking for Love* and *When Depression Hurts Your Relationship*

Finally, the guide to attracting your perfect partner is here! *The Practical Guide to Men* is the only book you'll need in your quest to find lasting love—it is the one book to help you find and keep the one. Dr. Smith provides an empathetic voice and skills that work, no matter what your relationship status is. If you want to heal the pain from the past, improve your current relationship, or gain the tools to attract the best guy for you, then pick up this book now!

—**Emily Roberts, MA,** author of theguidancegirl.com and *Express Yourself*

Good men abound—yes, really! But do you believe you deserve them? Do you know how to identify Mr. Right, and how to avoid Mr. Wrong? Whether you've picked inappropriate partners in the past, or whether you want to avoid them in your future, this book is for you. Based on science rather than opinion, and providing detailed examples that underscore every point, *The Practical Guide to Men* is definitely worth it.

—**Duana C. Welch, PhD,** author of *Love Factually*

The Practical Guide to Men

How to Spot the Hidden Traits of Good Men and Great Relationships

Shawn T. Smith, PsyD

mesa
PRESS

Published in Denver, Colorado, by Mesa Press, a division of
Mesa Psychological Services, Inc.
4045 Wadsworth Blvd., Suite 200
Wheat Ridge, CO 80033

Designed by Tracy Kimball Smith
Edited by Jean Blomquist

ISBN 978-0-9906864-2-2 (paperback)
ISBN 978-0-9906864-3-9 (electronic book)
Library of Congress Control Number: 2015913713
Version 1.1

CONTENTS

INTRODUCTION

Who delivered your formal training on romantic relationships? Who was your venerable sensei at the Academy of Love?

If you're like me and most of the people I meet, the answer is *no one*. Someone probably taught you how to solve for x, how to change a tire, and how to cook a delightful scrambled egg. But when it comes to one of life's most consequential decisions—choosing the person with whom to share that delightful egg—most of us are left to our own devices.

And so in the absence of formal training, we follow the examples set by our role models. That's a reasonable approach with mixed results. If our role models chose healthy, delightful relationships, then we're off to a great start! If not, we're in danger of replicating their relationships even if doing so fills us with pain and disappointment.

Let me introduce you to Rosa. She was twenty-five when I met her, and she was befuddled about whether she should marry the man who had recently proposed to her. Some part of her wanted to tie the knot because he seemed ideal on the surface. But the more cautious side of her knew something wasn't right.

Her ambivalence was understandable. On one side of the ledger, he possessed wonderful strengths. Her family liked him, he had plenty of friends, a lucrative job, and he was great with kids.

On the other side were serious shortcomings. Most prominent on that list was a jealous and controlling streak. He would secretly track her phone calls and text messages. He disapproved of her friends, sometimes insisting "it's them or me" when their desires conflicted with his. On several occasions, he had berated her when he felt jealous or injured.

I asked Rosa an audacious question when she described the unkind and ill-mannered side of his personality: "Are you aware good men don't behave that way?"

She gave me a puzzled look and thought for a long moment before answering, "No... I didn't know that."

Rosa simply had little experience with virtuous men or happy relationships because few of the men or women in her life had set positive examples. Their relationships had included various mixes of substance abuse, infidelity, ineffective communication, and plain old crabbiness. Her role models were good people who were unskilled at closeness and affection.

When she started dating as a teenager, Rosa chose relationships that emulated what her elders had shown her. None of them ended well. Now, at twenty-five, all those lackluster romances she had seen and participated in left her with a blind spot. She couldn't recognize when she was being treated poorly.

Fortunately, Rosa was willing to listen to the nagging little voice warning her about her prospective fiancé. As attractive as he was, she realized those jealous, controlling behaviors weren't going to improve on their own.

Who we choose to surround ourselves with is one of the most significant decisions in life. My years as a clinical psychologist have taught me that, among other reasons for choosing poorly, people often settle for familiarity or convenience when choosing their most significant relationships.

Some people are taken in by relationship charlatans. Some are in a hurry to fill what seems like an intolerable void of loneliness. Some people rush into relationships hoping to solve secondary problems like financial troubles. A few are even drunk or high when making life-altering choices. (Rarely a solid strategy.)

Despite the many reasons for choosing poorly, no one sets out to do so. No one resolves to find the partner who will leave her emotionally bruised and battered. We make the best decisions we can with the information at our disposal, whether we have too little experience or too many negative experiences. Rosa had a mix of both.

While she sensed a problem with the relationship, she couldn't quite identify it. Was his jealousy a normal reflection of his love, or was it more ominous? Her training hadn't prepared her to answer that question. She simply had a vague feeling that something was wrong, and she was smart enough to slow down and assess the situation. Heeding her intuition may have spared her from years of heartache.

It is rarely the job of a clinical psychologist to offer personal opinions, but I think it would have been a mistake for Rosa to marry this man. Perhaps he would have grown and changed over time, but my experience says it is unlikely. Men who treat women badly at the beginning of a relationship tend to get worse with time. (The same is true of women who treat men badly.) In all likelihood, this man's premarriage behavior was as good as it would ever be.

Two Ways to Choose the Wrong Man

Searching for the ideal mate is a little bit like searching for the ideal employee. The bad ones don't always look bad during a hasty interview, and the good ones don't always look good. Even the least-qualified applicant can write an exemplary resume and maintain a competent facade long enough to land the position, while the ideal candidate is sabotaged by a case of the jitters.

You may have noticed that the most confident and comforting men sometimes turn out to be the worst relationship material. Meanwhile, some of the best relationship prospects are easy to overlook, just like the best employees. And here's a cruel twist: the more smitten a good man is with you, the likelier he is to become a jittery doofus in your presence. The perfect man might be the one who unintentionally pushes you away.

There are the two basic errors women make when choosing the wrong men. They happen to be the same types of errors men make when choosing the wrong women, the same errors employers make when hiring the wrong people, and the same errors researchers make when confirming the wrong hypothesis. So please don't buy into feelings of shame if you've made these mistakes. You're in good and plentiful company.

The first is incorrectly assuming he's a good match when he isn't. Maybe you were taken in by the flashy guy who turned out to be a dud, or you chose someone whose relationship dynamic was familiar and comfortable, but ultimately unhealthy. Or maybe you both had the best of intentions, but you simply weren't compatible. Whatever the reason, the sooner you can detect this type of error, the quicker you can each get on with your lives and find your ideal mates.

The second type of error is to incorrectly reject an ideal match. This can happen when people like Rosa have difficulty recognizing a promising prospect. She overlooked many good men en route to the one who mistreated her because she didn't know how good men conduct themselves. Their behavior toward her was foreign and uncomfortable.

This second type of error also happens when an otherwise superb man is unskilled at dating. He might make a wonderful partner, but he doesn't know how to communicate that he's available and interested.

Rosa's dating history was a combination of both errors. She chose the wrong men and rejected the right ones. Her relationship compass was damaged, thanks largely to the people who should have taught her about healthy relationships. When she encountered good men who would have treated her well, she assumed they were operating on a different wavelength. She didn't know how to relate to them, so she didn't view them as relationship options.

For people like Rosa who were shortchanged in the role-model department, happy relationships seem like elusive specters in an unseen world. But it doesn't need to be that way.

WHERE ARE THE GOOD MEN?

Rosa wanted to be in a happy, healthy marriage. Her lack of experience with good men meant she simply needed to learn a bit about them. She also hadn't yet discovered how much *she* offered in a relationship, and that good men were looking for her.

Allow me to take a moment to define the term "good men." There are probably as many definitions as there are people to write them. For our purposes, I'll define a good man as one who possesses the skills, temperament, and desire to be successful in a long-term, romantic relationship.

You might be picking up this book because you're despairing what seems to be a shortage of good men, just as Rosa once did. In truth, the world is full of men who want happy, healthy relationships. In the service of finding them, we'll look at two main questions, beginning with this one:

What history, patterns, and values do you bring to relationships?

This book isn't just about good men, it is also about *you*. In part 1, we will examine your history with men, what you have learned to expect from relationships, and how your personal values affect your relationships with men. A solid understanding of your own relationship tendencies will help you clear the path for the best possible relationships with men.

Our second overarching question puts the focus squarely on men:

What makes men successful at long-term relationships?

It doesn't matter whether a man is liberal or conservative, religious or atheistic, a poet or a lumberjack. There are certain skills and qualities that, in my experience as a psychologist, help men succeed in relationships. To begin with, relationship-ready men possess three characteristics:

- sense of purpose
- good mental health
- emotional maturity

These are the three pillars of a good, relationship-ready man. Think of them as the minimum requirements for relationship success. That's the topic of part 2. Whether you're searching for a new romance or examining an existing one, learning the three pillars will help you weed out the immature or unhealthy men who cannot be fully present in a relationship so you can make room for the good men who deserve your attention and love.

Finally, we'll conclude with the 12-point man inspection in part 3. These twelve questions will help you assess a man's character, his capacity for devotion, and his relationship skills.

Along the way, we'll examine plenty of cautionary tales of men to avoid. More importantly, we'll illuminate the traits and behaviors that help men succeed in relationships. I'll show you what good men look like so you can avoid wasting time with those who aren't yet, or may never be, relationship material.

Our friend Rosa hadn't seen or experienced satisfying relation-ships, but she came to understand and appreciate her own history and strengths, and she discovered what a good, relationship-ready man could bring to her. With a bit of work, she was soon inviting the right kind of men into her world. Life is too short for anything less, so let us begin!

Part I
Why Good Men and Women Don't Find Each Other

Good men are everywhere. So why are they hard to find? Well, some good men don't know how to approach women. And some women don't know how to recognize good men. It's as if there is a wall between the most compatible people.

Don't despair if you're among those who have difficulty recognizing good men. You can't train men to market themselves more effectively, but you can learn how to find hidden gems.

The first step is a quick self-check. Before we approach the topic of fellas, let us make sure your own history and beliefs aren't clouding your view.

CHAPTER 1
YOUR HISTORY WITH MEN

If you asked a hundred professors to describe the history of men, you'd get a hundred different lectures. Some would be flattering; some would be critical. Each would mix reality with bias, and plenty would be inflated with five-dollar words.

We'll skip the professors, because there's only one version of history that matters in this book: *yours*. Before you and I ever crossed paths on these pages, influential men in your life shaped your perspective. They were fathers, brothers, family friends, teachers, fellow students, coworkers, and men who only passed you on the street or at the grocery store. Even if the important ones were absent or unavailable, their shortcomings made their mark on your personal history of men.

Men didn't do this alone. The women in your life also shaped your views, whether they admired men or viewed them with contempt. You probably watched as those women responded to the pain and joy men brought to their lives. Your mind undoubtedly took copious notes, eventually arriving at firm opinions about men. It probably offers sturdy opinions about men before you have a chance to discover their true character. That's what human minds do.

There's an old saying: understand history, or you're doomed to repeat it. That's never truer than in romantic relationships, which is why the first part of this book is about your history with men, and the core beliefs your mind has collected over the years. Core beliefs are enduring mental models of ourselves and our relationships. They can be optimistic—like *I can generally trust the people who love me*—or painful—like *I'll never measure up to others*. For good or bad, core beliefs help us understand and predict relationships.

Suppose you're at a restaurant and an attractive stranger approaches your table. Should you be wary of him? Indifferent? Curious? Does he remind you of someone who once treated you well? Is he reminiscent of a villain who treated you poorly? Core beliefs are lenses through which we answer these questions. They are the unwavering filters through which we view the world. They shape our emotional reactions, which in turn shape our choices.

Core beliefs are generally quite handy. We can examine any unfamiliar situation under the crisp template of well-established articles of faith, and quickly gain our bearings in unfamiliar territory. Any time you interact with a man, or travel to a new city, or encounter a stranger in the grocery store, your mind will offer up guiding thoughts and emotions filtered through history and core beliefs.

There are also drawbacks to core beliefs. First, our minds tend to overgeneralize.

Suppose a man you've never met approaches you at the grocery store. He reminds you of someone, yet he's unique. When the mind encounters a vaguely familiar situation, it has a tendency to say, *Eh, close enough. I'll lump this guy in with the others he reminds me of.* It will offer an opinion about the stranger—possibly a strong one—even though it has absolutely no experience with that individual.

A brief aside about the mind. Before we continue with the stranger in the grocery store, please indulge me in a brief aside. I frequently refer to "the mind" as if it's a separate entity. It isn't. But the brain is modular in design, with different areas performing different jobs.

Most of those areas are beyond our influence, though we still receive messages from them by way of sensations, memories, urges, and emotions. Because of the brain's modularity, it can seem like the mind is talking to us. It is, in its own way.

It can be useful to think of the mind as separate (even though it isn't) because doing so creates a bit of distance and freedom from our own thoughts and feelings. That distance creates insights we might not otherwise develop.

For example, it's challenging to notice the mind's repetitive thoughts. It's like a TV station running the same train wreck footage or storm forecast over and over. We can get sucked into the story and forget that we just watched it two minutes ago. But if we gain enough distance from the mind to notice that it is stuck on reruns, we can ask why it is repeating itself. And when we ask why, intriguing answers sometimes come to light. It all begins with the practice of viewing the mind from a safe distance.

If you are curious to read more about the mind's behavior, why it does what it does, and how to gain a bit of freedom from it, I invite you to read my book *The User's Guide to the Human Mind* (2011), though it certainly isn't a prerequisite for our discussion.

From here on, I'll use "the mind" as shorthand for the brain's modularity, with all of the thoughts and feelings it throws our way. I'll speak about the mind as if it is a separate entity, constantly whispering in our ears and pushing us in directions it thinks are best for us.

Now back to the mystery man in the grocery store—the one who seems vaguely familiar. In an instant, the moment you cross paths with him, your mind will call up core beliefs shaped by experience. Those experiences will coalesce into an emotional reaction that guides your response to him. Maybe your mind says *watch out, stay away*. Or maybe the man evokes feelings of comfort and safety.

The judgement is effortless. And it can be a real time-saver, even if it is inaccurate and misinformed. Thanks to core beliefs, you can quickly return to finding the best head of romaine lettuce rather than spending time contemplating the stranger.

From day one, we begin building a set of core beliefs about the workings of the world and other people. Your mind was compiling them long before you began considering romance, and the most important beliefs probably developed early.

Suppose, for example, that all goes well in an infant's life and she learns to trust parents as a source of nurturance. She develops a core belief that her parents will satisfy her needs. She doesn't need to learn it anew each time she feels hungry, hurt, or lonely. That core belief frees her to spend time learning about the world rather than worrying about food, warmth, and love. Without it, she might become preoccupied with a more distressing belief like *important people will let me down*.

Those old, deeply held beliefs can have profound effect in our adult lives. Let me tell you about Michelle. Her early experiences with men were mixed, leaving her with ambivalent beliefs about romance and about herself.

MICHELLE'S LONELINESS AND THE POWER OF CORE BELIEFS

Michelle's core beliefs started forming before she was born. Her mother had grown up to believe men should treat women well, an outlook that shaped Michelle's views and had a deep effect on her own relationships with men.

Michelle's parents met in college. Her mother was immediately taken not only with her father's handsomeness and intelligence, but with the gentlemanly way his parents had instilled in him. He was a kind and decent man. Michelle's brother, Jim, was born shortly after the marriage. He was two years her senior.

The early years were idyllic. The good man Michelle's mother had chosen turned out, unsurprisingly, to be an ideal father. He made a point to be home after work each day in time to eat dinner with the family and to play with the children. Aside from the occasional outing with friends, he devoted all of his free time to family and was a steady presence who could always make his children laugh.

One tragic day just after her tenth birthday, Michelle's father was killed in a car accident. The most prominent and positive male relationship of her young life ended in an instant.

The family idealized him after his death. They focused on the good times and inflated his already positive image. This idealized image made her even more proud he had been her father, and it also increased her distress about his absence. Throughout her teen years, she mourned the loss and wished he had been there to guide her, to make her laugh like he used to.

Her brother, Jim, would occasionally attempt to fill the gap left by their father. He would use his father's tools to make valiant if unsound attempts at repairs. He acted overly protective and paternalistic. In their teenage years, he made ham-fisted efforts to counsel Michelle in the ways of men, and he acted as an un-welcome chaperone whenever Michelle wanted a few hours alone with her friends. His efforts to replace his father were well inten-tioned, though they frequently tested the patience of Michelle and her mother.

When Michelle was fourteen, her mother began dating a co-worker. He was a virtuous man like their father, but the relation-ship didn't last. Michelle was growing close to this man, but unfor-tunately their friendship faded away when he left. It was another stinging loss. She sometimes experienced the dark thought that she had driven him away.

Despite her losses, Michelle had uneventful dating experiences in high school and college. She tended to pick kind, dependable boyfriends. Relationships came and went, as is typically the case early in life. She had a few relationships in her twenties, which each lasted a year or so.

By her early thirties, Michelle was tired of dating and wanted to settle down. This was when her core beliefs about men began to fully emerge and impede her ability to commit to a man. Now that she was more serious about dating, and the stakes were higher, she found it difficult to last more than a few months in a relationship.

Michelle had justifiably become fearful of abandonment after the loss of her father, the departure of her mother's boyfriend, and her own burgeoning string of failed relationships. She had developed the belief that relationships with men would always be incomplete and disappointing. That distressing thought lived deep in her psyche, like a dark cloud, and it drove her away from men.

In an attempt to explain the world, the human mind will sometimes turn on itself, as Michelle's mind did. Since logic couldn't explain the terrible losses she had experienced, she began to assume she was unworthy of being loved. That kind of core belief rarely shows itself in plain words. Michelle was simply left with the vague, dismal fear of being somehow damaged and undeserving.

Ironically, her painful core belief came about as a way of avoiding pain. By presuming she was unworthy of love, she would never be too surprised or injured when relationships failed. That was her mind's solution to a predicament that seemed beyond her control.

A pattern developed in her dating relationships. She would choose admirable men, fall in love quickly, and idealize them, much like her family had idealized her deceased father. But she repeatedly sabotaged herself. Fearing that a man might leave at any time, and thinking herself damaged, she vacillated between aloofness and desperation. The men in her life were often left feeling confused about what she wanted, and relationships routinely fizzled out. Sometimes her boyfriends broke up with her; sometimes she broke it off because she sensed the end approaching and hoped to minimize the pain.

The more her core belief played itself out, the more ingrained and habitual it became. Core beliefs are like a musical skill. The more we practice, the more automatic they become.

Michelle's story has a happy ending. She developed an understanding of the history and beliefs that had been driving her behavior and ruining her relationships, and in doing so created choices. She learned to listen to her core beliefs when they were helping her, and disregard them when they were working against her. Her relationships improved with this insight. Putting words to her beliefs helped her recognize when they were driving her behavior, and that moment-to-moment awareness enabled her to make different choices.

When she caught herself idealizing a new flame, she could remind herself to make a more realistic appraisal of the man. When she found herself fearing that the relationship was ending, she could question the thought rather than hastily reacting to it. And when she found herself feeling unworthy of love, she could remind herself that the feeling was an echo of distant events rather than a truth to be heeded. Such options didn't exist before she came to understand how her core beliefs influenced her behavior toward men.

THOSE PESKY, PROTECTIVE CORE BELIEFS

There are two things to know about core beliefs. First, they almost always exist to help us. Second, we don't always have to listen to them.

The mind always tries to protect us, even when it leads us away from what we most desire. Michelle wanted a solid, long-term relationship with a good man, but her mind had other plans. It wanted to insulate her from the pain of another abandonment. It prevented her from getting too close, which only served to create more abandonment.

The mind is great at churning out irony, like when it tells you to stay relaxed in a tense situation, but the idea of relaxing only serves to make you nervous. Thanks a lot, mind.

Michelle's mind actually helped create the pattern she so desperately wanted to escape. It became part of the problem it was trying to protect her from. For the longest time, she simply couldn't get past her mind's primal, emotional message. *This relationship is going to fail because you don't deserve lasting love,* it told her. *You're not good enough. He's going to leave if he truly gets to know you.*

It was all so inaccurate and unnecessary, but it was reality to some corner of Michelle's mind. It pushed her toward safety by seeking short-term comfort rather than long-term rewards. That's because the emotion-driven mind doesn't care a whit about tomorrow. It's interested in safety today. While part of her wanted to pursue relationship, another part wanted to escape the risk of pain. She was caught in the middle, bouncing between her emotions like a ping-pong ball.

Hers was not an unusual experience. Adults who experienced inconsistent nurturing (Michelle was both loved and abandoned) often experience an approach-avoidance dilemma in relationships (Mansfield and Cordova 2007). Michelle craved nurturing and closeness, while simultaneously she feared a repeat of the tremendous pain she felt when her father died. Whenever an intimate relationship developed, her mind became increasingly anxious. Eventually, the anxiety would overwhelm her and she would retreat.

Michelle's situation was not so different from the approach-avoidance dilemma of people who fear elevators. Anxiety increases as they move toward an elevator until they feel overwhelmed and compelled to retreat. Each time they retreat at the height of anxiety, the anxiety grows stronger.

Michelle's approach-avoidance dilemma was fueled by four core beliefs her mind had gathered about men:

- Relationships with men will always be incomplete and disappointing.
- I must constantly monitor relationships with men for signs of trouble.
- Good men leave when I need them most.
- I am unworthy of love.

These core beliefs were not necessarily correct or useful ways of thinking about men or herself, but Michelle's mind was only doing its job. It was gathering a history of painful events and protecting her from further injury.

It's like the elevator, but so much stronger. Because romantic relationships are so compelling and primal, our beliefs about the opposite gender can exert a tremendous influence on our behavior—even to the point of making us act like chowderheads in front of them. Once again: thanks a lot, mind.

Core beliefs can also twist our understanding of self and others. Michelle saw herself with an overly critical eye, while she idealized others. That particular combination of core beliefs has been tied to high degrees of distress, loneliness, and depression (Simard, Moss, and Pascuzzo 2011). It further impeded Michelle's romantic life by fueling general discomfort around the matter of romance.

Some people refer to Michelle's variety of beliefs as "maladaptive." I don't believe the mind adopts strategies it believes to be maladaptive. We wouldn't survive very long if it did. From the standpoint of Michelle's protective mind, her beliefs were perfectly reasonable. Her mind's approach to men made life safe and predictable. And the mind just *loves* safety and predictability. Michelle's core beliefs, as counterproductive as they were to her goals and desires, might have advanced her emotional safety in several ways:

- Assuming relationships with men would always be incomplete and disappointing prevented her from investing enough of herself to be deeply hurt again.

- Monitoring relationships for signs of trouble gave her an early warning system to help her avoid painful abandonment.

- Assuming men would leave her when she needed them prevented her from relying on men, decreasing her chances of disappointment.

- Even her false fear of being unlovable protected her in a strange way. It compelled her to act as if she were unlovable, which prevented men from getting close to her. *They can't abandon you if they can't get close*, said her mind.

Beliefs like these quickly outlive their usefulness, but they become self-fulfilling prophecies because we tend to find (or create) what we're looking for. While beliefs like Michelle's may insulate us from the anxiety of our own proverbial elevator, they can come with a tremendous long-term cost.

We all have our own core beliefs about the opposite sex. Some are useful, some are impediments to love and happiness. If we understand what our minds have learned about relationships, and if we understand when and why they are trying to protect us, we can make our own choices about obeying our thoughts and feelings. We can say good-bye to old ways of relating and open ourselves to the types of relationships we really want, even if it makes our minds uncomfortable. Discomfort fades when we understand the source and we're willing to sit with it in the service of creating something wonderful.

Michelle's core beliefs began with the most important people in her childhood: her parents. Fathers, in particular, carve the template for a girl's future relationships. Let's look at why fathers matter, and what to do if yours was absent or ineffective.

Why Fathers Matter

The importance of fathers, stepfathers, and other male role models is grossly understated in popular culture. TV and movies usually portray them as buffoons who pay the bills but otherwise contribute little to their children's well-being. In truth, fathers contribute tremendously to a child's development, particularly in the way girls learn to think about men.

For example, daughters report higher self-esteem and life satisfaction when their fathers are physically present and emotionally engaged. Teenagers with attentive fathers are less likely to engage in substance abuse. They possess better self-control, life skills, and social competence than those whose fathers were absent or disengaged. Women with loving and devoted fathers have higher levels of self-esteem; they are more independent and more successful. They have lower levels of anxiety and depression, and are generally more satisfied with their lives (Allgood, Beckert, and Peterson 2012).

At the other end of the spectrum, highly negative father-daughter relationships contribute to adult problems with self-concept, sexuality, and romantic relationships with men (Jones 2009).

In general, women possess better coping skills when their fathers offered warmth, structure, and respect for autonomy (as opposed to fathers who were rejecting, chaotic, or coercive). These women actually handle problems differently later in life. For example, when discussing social problems with their friends, women with warm fathers are less inclined to focus on uncontrollable or unpredictable elements. Instead, they focus on what they can control. They even experience less physical distress and healthier levels of cortisol, often called the stress hormone (Byrd-Craven et al. 2012).

Fatherhood is so crucial that it transcends divorce. Divorce doesn't necessarily impose long-term damage on a child's ability to have healthy adult relationships. Sometimes it is more important for a girl's parents to handle conflict constructively than it is to remain married.

Daughters tend to be more negatively affected later in life by high-conflict parents than are sons. Daughters are more prone to anxiety, depression, and a damaged self-image (Burns and Dunlop 2002). Whether or not parents divorce, daughters who have witnessed more destructive parental conflict are more fearful of intimacy than those who witnessed less conflict (Farbman 2002).

The women in a girl's life also affect her attitude toward men. A mother's trust in a girl's father affects the daughter's evaluation of him, which in turn affects her psychological well-being. The more a mother trusts the father, the more positively the daughter views her own relationship with him. Also, the mother's recognition of the father's supportive influence helps the daughter feel prouder of herself, happier, more satisfied, and less likely to feel depressed (Oshima 2009).

What about success in life and love? Fathers who are successful and who encourage academic achievement from their daughters positively influence their daughters' future career success (Gallagher 2008). The same researcher found that women who did not feel close to their fathers find it challenging to be close to men as adults. As women, they experience emotions similar to those their fathers evoked, including sadness, emptiness, and longing for deeper connections. Other influences aside, the quality of a girl's relationship with her father can predict both her career and romantic success.

Fathers don't need to be perfect. They simply need to be present, attentive, and maintain loving relationships with the women in their family. Women do better in life when their fathers have been warm and dependable.

Please don't let this discussion bring you down if your father was a weak or absent role model. I'm discussing father-daughter relationships to illuminate the challenges that may lie ahead of you, or the assets that sit in your favor, based on your father's performance as a parent. Even if he came up short, his influence need not be carved in stone.

Unfair though it is, some women need to work harder to make up for their fathers' lack of effort. But believe it or not, those s women may come out better for it. While positive experiences are a great start, painful experiences can make us stronger and wiser.

Some psychologists say we repeat old experiences in order to repair them, or to finally obtain what was missing, such as a caring father figure. Perhaps that's true. But there may be a simpler explanation: we do what we know how to do, what we're comfortable with, what we've been taught. We do it because it comes naturally. I like this explanation better because it means we can take charge and transcend our past.

Despite what popular culture tells us, most fathers do a great job. At the very least, most fathers are adequate. Others drop the ball or disappear entirely. Relationships are easier to navigate when we take an honest, realistic appraisal of the job our fathers did so we can understand the lessons they gave us, both useful and otherwise. I've noticed many people, men and women alike, are hesitant to recognize the damage caused by an absent or ineffective father. They can be equally hesitant to give praiseworthy fathers full credit for the positive contributions to their lives.

If your father was present and attentive, then take inventory of what he taught you. If your father and other male role models were less than stellar, you still have options aplenty. There are countless good men to bring into your life.

What to Do If Your Father Was Absent

If you were one of the far-too-many children who live without a father, this section is for you. His absence or defects need not impede your adult relationships. You can choose wonderful relationships even when you haven't been shown what they look like. Struggles and deprivations can strengthen anyone who's willing to do her emotional pushups.

Michelle, from earlier in the chapter, is a great example. Through no fault of her own, she began to repeat a cycle of unsuccessful relationships. As unfair as it was, she had to work harder at relationships and learn be more introspective than others. The effort gave her priceless insight into her own motivations, and a better understanding of relationships in general. In the spirit of Michelle's success, here are five tasks to help transcend absent fathers and poor male role models.

Know your history so you don't repeat it. In the previous section, we discussed the ways in which loving and attentive fathers affect their daughters. Let's review those now, and add a few more:

- Good fathers are physically present and emotionally engaged.
- They provide warmth, structure, and respect for autonomy.
- They help their kids develop problem-solving skills.
- They handle conflict productively.
- They have some measure of personal success, they have high expectations, and they encourage their children to succeed.
- Their children feel close to them.
- They maintain positive and supportive relationships with their grown children.
- They maintain positive relationships with the women in their lives.

If your father came up short, it's useful to realistically appraise the way in which his shortcomings affected you. In my experience, people tend to either overstate or understate their parents' effectiveness. Both errors allow history to exert undue influence on our lives. Avoiding reality by understating history blinds us to the effect it has on our behavior. Exaggerating reality by overstating history binds us to its influence and encourages perpetual victimhood.

The antidote to both errors is a solid understanding of our core beliefs, those deeply-ingrained mental shortcuts that help us understand and predict relationships. Without that insight, we're left only with the winds of emotion filling our sails and pushing us toward the rocks. Emotions alone leave us few choices for new ways of behaving, but options increase dramatically when we aim our intellect and verbal skills at our inner workings.

One of the quickest and most efficient ways to identify core beliefs is to spend a few sessions with a skilled psychologist. There are also many resources to help uncover core beliefs, some offering structured journaling exercises. An online search for books about core beliefs or cognitive schemas is a good way to start searching for resources that might appeal to you. Even without structured guidance, plain old journaling is a powerful way to develop insight. Surround yourself with examples of satisfying, healthy relationships. Even if your parents were unhappy, you can still choose to associate with happy couples. Why reinvent the wheel when you can learn from their success? Study them. Talk to them about what works. Read about healthy relationships. Make it your job to become a relationship expert.

Even people who are blessed with successful relationship role models have to learn what works and forge their own path. Observing unsuccessful relationships creates useful knowledge about what *doesn't* work. You can combine that with lessons from successful couples about what *does* work.

When uncovering your core beliefs about men, be aware that skilled and loving fathers are sometimes ostracized or vilified by adult women in the family. That can unjustly taint a daughter's view of men in general. Anger between the genders transfers easily from one generation to the next, but you needn't adopt the anger that rightfully belongs to a predecessor. Let *that person* be miserable. You have a life to live.

Don't tolerate bad behavior or poor treatment.
People generally tolerate what they think they deserve in relationships, be it from bosses, friends, strangers, or romantic partners. If your upbringing left you with the impression that romantic relationships entail rudeness and mean-spiritedness, it's time to reject that lesson. Successful relationships have a foundation of respect, courtesy, reliability, and kindness. If those basic experiences were missing from your relationship training, it might feel uncomfortable to demand good treatment. Demand it anyway. The discomfort of high standards will fade.

Embrace relationship mistakes. Have you fallen into lousy relationships in the past? They may have been time well spent if you can identify your role in them as well as the core beliefs behind the decisions you regret.

Behave confidently in relationships, even if you don't feel like it. Prisoners and other wards of the state sometimes become so dependent on the rules and structure of the institution that they lose confidence in their ability to function outside its walls. When they lose confidence, they can begin acting as if they're helpless. When they begin acting as if they're helpless, then they start to believe independence is hopeless. A similar sense of hopelessness can develop around the idea of relationships.

We discussed earlier how a woman's confidence can suffer when her father abandoned, ignored, or mistreated her. His unfatherly behavior can lead to destructive core beliefs about her worthiness or the dependability of others. The institutionalized prisoner has bought into an illusion, and we make the same mistake when we buy into old, broken-down relationship beliefs.

The answer? Disobey those damaging beliefs. If your mind says you don't deserve to be treated well, act as if you do, whether you feel like it or not. If your mind says there are no good men, behave as if they are everywhere. Act as if they're looking for you, whether you believe it or not. If your mind says no man will love you once he gets to know you, disobey that thought. Act as if he will love you even more as he gets to know you.

Disobeying the mind can be uncomfortable because it tends to fight back with hefty doses of anxiety. But unhelpful thoughts and core beliefs are meant to be disobeyed. We become institutionalized by our own counterproductive thoughts when we behave as if they're true.

Carry Your History Lightly

It's both beautiful and troubling that minds record history whether we like it or not. With or without your knowledge or consent, it has probably decided to protect you from certain situations, or relationships, or types of men. Sometimes the mind is wise and correct; sometimes it overgeneralizes and blocks our desires.

The mind's fears are often an indication of what we want in a relationship. For example, a mind that protects its owner from abandonment usually desires attachment. Remember Michelle from the beginning of the chapter? For her mind, abandonment and attachment are two sides of the same coin. Her challenge is to carry the coin lightly, and because of its importance, to be exquisitely aware of its presence and its effect.

We can take power away from our history and our core beliefs when we put words to them. Below are a few questions to help you verbalize your history and pin down your core beliefs about men and relationships. Don't worry if you struggle with this exercise. It *is* challenging. Spend some time with these questions, journal about them, discuss them with a therapist. The time you spend uncovering your core beliefs now might prevent years of heartache.

I encourage you to spend time with these questions before going forward. People who read early versions of this book suggested it would be useful to keep a journal to record exercises and thoughts. I think they were on to a fine idea.

Know Your History

What did your parents teach you about relationships, both by words and by deed?

What did your father, and other men, teach you about how men think and behave?

What did your mother, and other women, teach you about men?

Who have been the most influential men in your life, for good or ill, and how have they shaped the way you think about relationships with men?

Which of your beliefs about men contribute to hurtful, unsatisfying relationships?

Which of your beliefs about yourself contribute to hurtful, unsatisfying relationships?

Which of your beliefs about men and yourself contribute to positive and satisfying relationships?

CHAPTER 2
YOUR HIDDEN RELATIONSHIP PATTERNS

Do you know what brings many people to the office of a clinical psychologist? They've grown weary of repeating their unproductive patterns. The underlying matter can be anything from weight loss to job performance. Often, it is relationships. They're tired of repeating the same old heartbreaks.

There's an old metaphor in psychology that says horses return to a burning barn because, as dangerous as the fire might be, the barn itself represents security at a stressful moment.

People and horses aren't so different. We're drawn to our old patterns—our proverbial burning barns—during our own stressful moments.

Predictability feels safe, and sometimes our patterns work out great. If you have a pattern of showing up to work early, or saving money for a rainy day, then you'll have an easier go of it than someone who doesn't have those patterns. Some patterns succeed more than others.

We're likelier to repeat the patterns we practice, whether or not they benefit us. It doesn't matter whether the pattern is useful, like arriving at work early, or a harmful, like dating the wrong kind of people.

There's yet another way in which patterns are similar to core beliefs: we can be blind to them until we describe them with words. Just as with core beliefs, putting words to our patterns creates choices.

Consider the cautionary tale of Colleen. Like the proverbial frightened horse, she returned to her old patterns at the worst moments, and she couldn't see the toll those patterns were taking.

Shy Colleen and the Power of Harmful Patterns

Colleen developed habits in childhood that harmed her adult romances, but she can hardly be blamed. You could say her patterns with men were a perfectly normal reaction to her childhood circumstances.

Colleen had always been shy by nature. As a child, she was gangly and clumsy, traits which some of her crueler classmates were quick to point out. Her self-consciousness made her standoffish toward boys. They didn't know how to respond to what seemed like aloofness, and so they teased her, as boys will do.

The more they teased her, the more awkward she felt—thus started her destructive cycle with men. At a young age, she began thinking boys would never be attracted to her. She felt boys had rejected her unfairly and permanently. Somewhere deep in the emotional recesses of her mind, she began to resent them.

She also began to resent herself. In junior high school, a prominent set of braces added to her awkward appearance and pushed her even further away from boys. And because she wasn't interacting with them, she wasn't learning about them. (If only she had known how many other kids were experiencing similar insecurities!)

Unlike school, life at home was agreeable. Colleen's parents and two older sisters were solid and reliable. Dinnertime was lively and fun. Normal sibling friction notwithstanding, Colleen enjoyed time with her family.

Looking back as an adult, she realized she had sometimes been lost in the shuffle. Her sisters were wrapped up in their own lives, and her busy parents assumed no news was good news. They never noticed Colleen struggling with self-image, and she never thought to tell them. The absence of assistance from her otherwise happy and helpful family contributed to her belief that she was undesirable.

Had the adults in her life offered a bit of help, high school might have been a turning point. Boys began to take an interest in her as she grew into her body and outgrew her braces. Their attention was foreign to her. It was overpowered by the outdated thought that she was gangly and unattractive. Like most of us, she acted on her thoughts rather than the reality around her. Even though her reality had changed, she remained standoffish and awkward with boys.

She went on a few dates, but she was so preoccupied with her fear of being undesirable that she unintentionally pushed the boys away. They found her to be cold and aloof, despite her desire to connect with them. Yet again, her mistaken belief that men found her repulsive was falsely confirmed, and her awkward behavior around young men was becoming her standard.

Her self-critical beliefs and her standoffish behaviors remained even through college, though she became more polished in her presentation. Her work-study position with the college IT department forced her to interact with people, but only briefly and on a surface level.

Her job came with some clout and authority, and she learned how to be charismatic. She replaced her wall of shyness with a wall of social charm, but still never really connecting with men. She was more outgoing on the surface, but she still held men at a distance. Her pattern of avoiding men had become entrenched, and it was beginning to cost her a great deal.

Colleen began to notice the pattern by her late twenties. She realized that she had been lonely in all of her romantic relationships, but she didn't quite understand why. She'd had a series of boyfriends who had all seemed shallow and uninvolved. She hadn't yet identified the role she played in choosing those men. By keeping them at a distance and never really opening up to them, she naturally attracted men who were comfortable with relationships of little depth.

For example, in college she chose to date a man whose energies went mainly to pot and video games. He was a virtual escape artist, managing to vanish emotionally whenever he was needed. They drifted apart when she had to deal with the death of a family member. True to his nature, he retreated into his bong and his game console when she needed him most.

Her next relationship was with a coworker who was gregarious, motivated, and quite busy. While she admired him more than the pot-addicted man she had previously dated, there was something empty about the relationship. He, too, managed to escape whenever she began to delve beyond surface-level conversations. Rather than vanishing into a marijuana-induced haze, this man disappeared into his work.

Still she did not recognize she was choosing distant, emotionally isolated men who only participated to the level she thought she was worthy of. Her next major relationship, with a man named David, was one more iteration of the pattern.

She met David at a friend's wedding as she approached her thirty-fourth birthday. He was career-driven and worked long hours. When he wasn't working, he was courting clients at social functions. Colleen and David spoke on the phone most days, but never for more than a few minutes, and never with the closeness that Colleen craved.

She moved in with David, hoping to establish more togetherness and intimacy. He returned from work each night exhausted and in no mood to converse. Occasionally, they would open a bottle of wine and watch a movie together in silence. But even then she felt no emotional closeness with him.

Weekends involved client-centered activities in which she never felt she had his full attention. If he wasn't with clients, he would often simply abandon her to bike or golf with friends. Even during the occasional Sunday evenings when they were alone, he seemed intent on keeping the conversation at a surface level.

She had reached a point in her life when she wanted more. She wanted to settle down, but not with David or anyone like him. She felt lonelier in this relationship than she ever had before. He moved out after a tense breakup, and she sometimes saw him in their circle of mutual friends. Her mind interpreted the breakup as one more indication of a failing romantic life.

The bitterness she began to feel toward men as a child had grown into a jaded sense that she could never be happy with men. Her only explanation was the simplistic, blanket judgment that men are shallow. She was blaming them for her loneliness.

Colleen had lost sight of the fact that only *some* men are shallow, and she was going out of her way to choose those men because they fit her core belief that she was unworthy of an attentive man. Having had a disagreeable start with boys through no fault of her own, she had unwittingly created her own entrenched pattern of loneliness.

Pattern Blindness

Colleen was not a bitter person by nature, yet she came to bitterly blame men for her loneliness. Far from being a shortcoming or character flaw on her part, her conclusion made perfect sense from her mind's point of view.

Human minds are pattern-finding machines, and they *love* to devise explanations for those patterns. Unfortunately, our minds can easily overgeneralize and oversimplify in their search for an explanation. That's why we need to keep a close eye on them.

If you'll recall Michelle from chapter 1, her mind turned to self-blame to explain her painful experiences with men. *I'm flawed, and no man could ever like me if he really knew me.*

Colleen had a similar core belief, but rather than overgeneralizing about herself, she overgeneralized about men: *I'll never be able to love a man because they all are shallow and obtuse.* By acting on her mind's overgeneralization, she unintentionally created experiences to confirm it.

Our worrying, protective, pattern-finding mind has a natural tendency to internalize misfortunes and disproportionately blame ourselves, or externalize them and disproportionately blame others. In reality, the true source of problems is usually some combination of our experiences and our choices. Colleen's experiences started her down a path of choices that led her to oversimplify the male mind.

Men do tend to talk less and handle intimacy differently than women, which is different from shallowness. In *The Woman's Guide to How Men Think*, I surveyed hundreds of men who explained that while men may be more stoic than women, good men—even the quiet ones—still desire a deep connection with a woman.

Still, there are plenty of shallow men out there, and Colleen's core beliefs compelled her to find a string of them through no real fault of her own, since her motivations were largely beyond her awareness.

But we all have to grow up and take responsibility at some point. Colleen eventually realized she had lost sight of the common denominator: her own actions. *She* had been overlooking men of depth and choosing the men her mind expected her to find.

She had stumbled into one of her mind's survival strategies. As her discomfort and sadness increased over time, her mind was like the horse running to a burning barn. It insisted that she keep repeating her earliest, strained, and distant experiences with boys. While certainly not fun or comfortable, those interactions were at least familiar and predictable.

This is yet another trick of an overprotective mind. It often values predictability over success. Colleen knew how to conduct herself in shallow relationships, and she knew how to find them. Predictability insulated her from the hard work of finding true romance.

In short, Colleen's mind was doing a bang-up job of protecting her from something it believed to be exotic, dangerous, and beyond reach: intimacy with a good man. Luckily, she caught on before life passed her by.

Hand-Me-Down Patterns

Here's another sneaky little secret about patterns. They can pass from one generation to the next like old family photos, and our beliefs about the reliability of intimate relationships can be a distant echo of our parents' experiences with emotional attachment. Kilmann and colleagues (2009) looked at ninety young women with married parents and found that the positive and the negative experiences of one generation—especially the mother's—can affect the relationships of the next.

Suppose, for example, a girl's mother is distrustful of men. Maybe she prefers emotional distance and dismisses intimacy. Or maybe painful experiences taught her to distrust close relationships. Perhaps experience had given her mixed feelings about closeness, leaving her uncertain about the reliability of relationships. Her desire for intimacy might be overshadowed by fear about her partner's fidelity and her own worthiness. If she's not careful, she will pass those beliefs to her daughter.

In the Kilmann study, those mothers who were dismissive, insecure, or uncertain about relationships tended to have daughters who were—you guessed it—also dismissive, insecure, or uncertain about relationships. These types of mothers had a greater tendency to use harmful ways of controlling their daughters, such as guilt, possessiveness, and withdrawing affection. It was especially harmful when both the mother *and* father shared a similar, insecure view of attachment.

On the other hand, parents who felt secure in relationships were more accepting of their daughters' individuation, they were less controlling, had better parenting skills, were more involved, and were more consistently affectionate with their daughters. The daughters of these parents were likelier to feel safe and secure in their adult relationships. There's wonderful news in this study. Healthy relationship habits appear to be more reliably transmitted to the next generation than unhealthy ones (though the unhealthy habits also got handed down like an ugly pair of bell-bottom jeans).

What's the lesson in all this? In order to understand our own romantic tendencies, it helps to understand how our parents viewed emotional intimacy. Their relationship style influences ours, but their choices are not our destiny. The more knowledge we have about our own inner workings, and how we arrived at them, the more easily we can make our own decisions about relationships.

THANK YOUR MIND: IT'S ONLY TRYING TO HELP

Back to Colleen. As comforting as it might have been to blame men for her loneliness, Colleen was ultimately the common denominator. *Her* beliefs and *her* grown-up choices led to a string of shallow, unreliable boyfriends.

I don't wish to be hard on Colleen. Her choices were logical from standpoint of a normal, protective mind. The mind's defensive functions lie beneath the surface, beyond our control. Colleen's mind had erroneously gathered that pursuing interesting, attentive men would only cause pain.

Shallow, unreliable relationships were at least predictable. People and even animals generally prefer predictable punishment over unpredictable pain. Colleen's mind didn't explain to her *why* it was preventing her from choosing reliable relationships with good men. It simply pushed her in familiar directions to minimize her suffering.

As a young girl, Colleen's shy mind learned to avoid scrutiny and rejection the same way it learned to avoid touching a hot stove. It wordlessly moved her away from situations in which she might experience scrutiny and rejection. She would have been the last girl in the world to sign up for a talent show or a team activity. Those activities would have put too many eyes on young Colleen.

From her adult mind's point of view, choosing shallow, unreliable men was a perfect solution. The men she chose would never scrutinize her too closely because they were incapable or uninterested in doing so. She would never be rejected for who she really was.

Plus, inattentive men never really made her happy. There was a strange advantage in that. If she avoided attentive and virtuous men, she minimized the risk of losing happiness, because it had never really existed. It didn't count as rejection or failure when flimsy relationships fell apart.

We can't blame our minds for trying to keep us safe. Sometimes it is easier to simply express gratitude for these worry machines.

But gratitude for our minds doesn't mean we need to obey them. We can choose our own path when we know what the sneaky little bundles of nerves are up to, and why they sometimes make such counterproductive choices.

WHY THE MIND IS PRONE TO TERRIBLE RELATIONSHIP DECISIONS

Inaccurate core beliefs can put loving relationships out of reach. Colleen's experience showed us how we can adopt relationship patterns that create precisely the types of relationships we *don't* want.

There's one more important way in which the mind can set us up for unhealthy relationships. Left to its own devices, the human mind approaches relationship choices the same way a child approaches dietary choices: pretty candy is more appealing than a nutritious meal.

Mate selection is a complex topic, to make an obvious point. People have devoted entire careers to deciphering the occasionally inscrutable decisions people make regarding their love lives. Here's one of the more common findings: the mind generally draws our attention to attractive short-term mates who might be utterly incompatible with us in the long run. It doesn't seem to have gotten the memo that we hope to spend a lifetime with this person.

Ideally, we would take the time to peer into each prospective mate's soul before committing to that person, but that can take years. The primitive, emotional side of the human mind seems to be in a mighty rush, and so it points us toward people who look like shiny pennies on the outside, even if they are rusted and tarnished on the inside.

The primitive emotional mind can be downright clueless when it comes to picking mates. Other factors aside, the male mind tends toward physical attractiveness as the measure of a woman's relationship fitness; the female mind tends toward social competence as the measure of a man.

I think it's rare that people follow their mind's facile approach to dating (unless they are quite drunk), but still it is a powerful motive that figures prominently in our choices. Relying on surface characteristics is an efficient way to quickly procreate, if you're inclined to follow your mind down such a reckless path. It is also a lousy recipe for successful, long-term relationships. The person who seems ideal on the surface, where the primitive mind is focused, can be a relationship train wreck waiting to happen.

There are real costs to the mind's short-term strategy. Research has shown that women who openly and intentionally seek short-term relationships are relatively inattentive to factors like intelligence, social skills, and personal success—qualities that contribute to long-term relationships success—whereas women who aim for long-term relationships are far more attracted to those more subtle factors (Goetz 2013).

According to the same findings, women seeking short-term relationships place more importance on "sex appeal, muscularity, physical attractiveness, facial masculinity, and immediate displays of resources." Short-term goals make us less discriminating, leaving women more likely to sacrifice noble character for an attractive surface.

I don't mean to suggest there's anything wrong with short-term relationships, though I suspect anyone reading this book is striving for a long-term partnership. That puts us somewhat at odds with our own short-term motivated minds. If the mind had its way, this would be the order of priorities in mate selection:

- First priority: shiny surface
- Second priority: goodness of fit

Following this recipe is like buying an automobile and then asking, "What kind of car should I get?" Maybe we luck out and that approach fetches the perfect match. Or maybe we're now stuck with a broken-down beater that looked great on the showroom floor. Now we have a larger quandary: what to do with this lemon?

If you'll pardon my candor, don't think you're not at risk of making shallow choices. We all are susceptible to the mind's pursuit of short-term satisfaction at the expense of long-term success. As the researchers above reported, "[W]omen may not always be consciously aware of, or willing to admit to, their mating interests...." In other words, many women venture into the dating scene without a goal, and when people have no goal, their minds can latch onto the first shiny object that captures their attention.

According to one set of highly respected researchers, women, more than men, use short-term strategies to "audition" men for long-term relationships (Buss and Schmidt 1993). That means the mind may be weeding out men of virtuous character in its search for attractive genetic features. It's as if the mind drags us to a car dealership that only sells the automobiles we don't want. It is blind to the more fitting dealership across the street.

It's normal to operate with blinders. Humans aren't predisposed to peering inside their own minds, and we're certainly reluctant to disobey the mind's impulses. The answer is not to try to eliminate or silence the mind, but rather to supervise it. We each have the ability to reorder our mind's shortsighted strategy so that it suits long-term goals:

- First priority: goodness of fit
- Second priority: shiny surface

If your mind has been searching for a compatible partner among the people you find most attractive, then maybe the more effective strategy is to turn that formula upside down. Search for the partner you find attractive among the people who are most compatible.

STRESS AND DATING

There's one more relevant facet of the protective mind. One of its most powerful motives is to eliminate pain, anxiety, and discomfort. Here, perhaps more than anywhere else, the primitive mind is driven by short-term considerations. What comes *later* doesn't matter if the mind can eliminate pain *now*. Pain relief compels the proverbial horse to run, not walk, into the burning barn.

When we are under stress, the need for safety and predictability becomes increasingly serious to most minds because reducing uncertainly reduces discomfort. Just as we can make poor dietary decisions when we're overly tired, we can make poor relationship decisions when we are lonely or hurting.

Old, unworkable patterns become particularly seductive when we're experiencing tough times, like relationship or work problems. Think of the recovering alcoholic who returns to the bottle at a low point in life, precisely when alcohol is the most destructive choice.

You can sometimes see this in people who have survived high-conflict divorces. If they neglect the emotional task of coming to terms with the loss of their marriage, along with the challenging task of identifying patterns that contributed to the divorce, then they are at high risk for falling into a new relationship in which they repeat the same old conflicts.

We can see the effect of stress-based decision making in divorce statistics. Each time a person divorces, the likelihood they will divorce again in the future increases (Kreider and Ellis 2011). Undoubtedly, one of the biggest contributors to this statistic is a failure to examine old patterns. Those who haven't resolved the destructive patterns and behaviors that contributed to the first divorce are likely to carry them into the next marriage, where their inevitable pain will drive them back to familiar, dysfunctional patterns. It's a terrible double whammy. The mind's attempt to reduce discomfort through old, familiar patterns can leave us even more mired in the pain we're trying to avoid.

It doesn't have to be that way. People who study their patterns, taking care to identify their role in them, can easily defy statistics.

Reclaiming Your Future

Wouldn't you like to have a time machine that would tell you what your future relationships will look like? Well, I have good news. You already have one! It exists in the patterns of your past decisions. Tomorrow's relationships will resemble yesterday's unless you challenge those old patterns and reclaim your future.

Left on its own, the mind will repeat history and rehearse your core beliefs like a broken record. One of the first steps in changing them is to remove the "good" and "bad" labels we attach to them. Patterns aren't our friends or enemies, they're just helpful or unhelpful in pursuit of our goals. After all, the roots of our patterns are rarely of our choosing, and even the most unhelpful patterns probably served us well at some time in our lives.

For example, consider the powerful effect of fathers. For better or worse, fathers help establish the foundation on which a woman's relationships are built. In addition to all we discussed earlier, fathers influence women's self-esteem, age of sexual activity, and whether they choose men who meet their needs (Del Russo 2010).

Though we don't choose the roots of our patterns, at some point we bear responsibility for them. Even when fathers do a miserable job, *we* eventually become the common denominator in our unsuccessful relationships if we don't challenge those early lessons. It is our job to intervene when the mind tries to replicate what it learned from our fathers, our mothers, or any other significant influence.

At the end of this chapter is a list of questions to help you identify the relationship patterns you have developed. As with the questions at the end of chapter 1, it's normal to struggle with this one. The mind doesn't easily divulge this sort of information. Here are some suggestions to help you get started.

Put words to the patterns. The mind has a tendency to do rather than deliberate. We can short-circuit that tendency by taking time to describe patterns, history, and core beliefs. Words create understanding, and understanding creates options.

Suppose you have a tendency to pick men who turn out to be cheaters. By putting words to the qualities, history, and types of interactions propelling you toward these men, you can catch your mind in the act as it steers you toward the next potential cheater. Maybe, for example, you're susceptible to a certain manner of sweet-talk from dishonest men. Putting words to that vulnerability creates choices as the patterns unfolds. You won't have to look back later and wondering why it happened again. What could be more freeing?

Journaling, talking with close friends and family, and working with a skilled psychologist are excellent ways to put words to patterns.

Identify the warning signs. After you have a clear understanding of the patterns you have fallen into, it's time to identify the little signs that indicate you're slipping down the same old slope. It's useful to think *large* when defining patterns, searching for overarching themes and behaviors that repeat over a period of weeks, months, or years. But it helps to think *small* when looking for the warning signs of pattern repetition.

Here's what I mean. Suppose a person possesses an overarching pattern of dating partners who are jealous and controlling. It can take years for each iteration of the pattern to play out as each relationship runs its course. Within each of those overarching patterns are small indications that the pattern is repeating.

For example, the next controlling partner (the large pattern) might show signs of jealousy early in the relationship (the small warning sign). He might express disapproval when his partner spends time with friends and family. Or he may pry into her cell phone or email records. The partner, in turn, may find herself ignoring the warning signs with excuses like *he's just worried.* Small behaviors like that kind of excuse making might indicate she is establishing a new relationship similar to the old ones.

We can break it down even further because, as obvious as those controlling behaviors in our example might seem in retrospect, they can be tough to detect in the moment. That's when it helps to identify the thoughts, emotions, and even physical sensations accompanying old patterns. In our example of the controlling partner, perhaps the jealous behaviors in the past have led to thoughts like *I better be careful not to arouse his suspicion right now*. Or maybe there were tiny pangs of trepidation, tightness in the chest, headaches, or other physical signals.

By putting words to the patterns and our reactions to them, we can train ourselves to recognize those little thoughts, emotions, and bodily sensations as warning signs. Those subtle, internal experiences can become like the little red dashboard lights on a car.

The check-engine light doesn't describe the nature of the problem. It merely tells you to stop and assess the situation before you damage the car. A physical sensation, a thought, or a little pang of emotion can do the same job as a dashboard warning light.

Slow the process. Slowing down is key to breaking destructive patterns. Sometimes we need a few minutes to turn off the autopilot and think about our next move.

For example, people who are trying to manage their diet profit by stepping away from the table for a few minutes before taking a second helping. Sensible decisions are easier when we remove ourselves from temptation. That's true of most any habit change, even relationship habits. Slowing down provides time to think, confer with friends, journal about the situation, and avoid a costly, impulsive decision.

Changing lifelong patterns can seem daunting at first, so it helps tremendously to think small. You have probably heard this old joke: "How do you eat an entire elephant? One bite at a time." Patterns show up in small, everyday decisions. As soon as you alert yourself to those little moments, you have already begun changing the pattern.

As with the previous chapter, please take your time with the questions below. The answers are sometimes slow to appear.

Know Your Patterns

*What similarities can you identify in men
you have dated or found attractive?*

*Which of your relationship patterns with men are worth repeating,
and what experiences are best left in the past?*

*Were there communication or relationship patterns you found to be
troubling or destructive between your parents?
What about positive patterns between them?*

*What communication patterns between you and your mother
did you find to be troubling? Which patterns were helpful?*

*What communication patterns between you and your father
did you find to be troubling? Which patterns were helpful?*

*Thinking back to past relationships with men, can you identify thoughts,
emotions, or bodily sensations that suggest a destructive pattern was
starting anew? Be sure to include the positive thoughts, feelings, and
sensations (especially that devilishly deceptive feeling of infatuation) as
well as the unpleasant feelings, thoughts, and sensations.*

CHAPTER 3
WHAT YOU CAN TRUST WHEN YOU CAN'T TRUST YOUR MIND

Imagine you had a magic compass steering you toward the right relationships even when your mind had other plans. It could tell you when you're about to drive off a relationship cliff, or when that nervous guy in front of you might be Mr. Right.

You already have that compass. It lies in your *values*: your judgment about what matters in life. A clearly defined set of values *is* the magic compass with the power to guide our most important decisions, even when our mind is up to its counterproductive shenanigans.

What matters to you? It seems like such an obvious question, but the finer points of our own values can be tough to pin down. I'll give you plenty of tools to help, beginning with our most important values-related question. You might add this to your journal, if you're keeping one:

What kind of romantic partner do you want to be?

This is no tedious, academic inquiry. If you know your values, then you can choose a similarly inclined man, and a similarly inclined man has a better chance of being a happily-ever-after man. Shared values matter tremendously in relationships.

For example, consider the causes of divorce. There are obvious factors like substance abuse and sexual incompatibility, but among the top reasons are factors directly related to incompatible values. Couples are likelier to divorce when they marry too young, or marry before their educations are complete, or when they are markedly dissimilar in age, educational attainment, or religion. Couples who spend less positive time with each other are also at higher risk for divorce (Lowenstein 2005).

Large demographic differences like age or religion frequently involve large differences in values. While relationships with disparate values can certainly work, it requires extra effort. It's easier to spend time with someone whose values we share, which may be one of the reasons similar values are a powerful predictor of marital satisfaction (Mckinley 1997).

Consider one of the most common sources of conflict among couples: money. Surprisingly, shared goals and values about money are a stronger predictor of relationship satisfaction than are communication strategies (Archuleta 2011).

Maybe that's because attitudes about money are a reasonable proxy for life priorities. I suppose the partner who wants to spend the family paycheck in Cancún will have tense discussions with the one who wants to sink it into blue-chip stocks. Compatibility on basic philosophies about life is more strongly related to happiness than even the words we use, and choosing a compatible man requires a thorough understanding of your own values.

Who Do You Want to Be?

Human minds are meddlesome little critters. Both Michelle and Colleen in our previous chapters wanted happy, fulfilling relationships. Their protective minds—with their collections of history, core beliefs, and patterns—had different plans. What are we to do when the mind is working against us?

Just like a solid understanding of our inner workings, a clear understanding of our own values helps mute the power of a mind pulling us away from what we want. Clear values aren't just a magic compass; they're rocket fuel for a successful life and happy relationship.

Sexy comes and goes, but values endure. Ideally, our partners share in our interests. At the very least, a compatible partner supports our interests from the sidelines. As our next couple painfully demonstrates, clashing values can create terrible strife.

Julia and Rob: A Case of Colliding Values

Julia and Rob met in college, where he was already well on his way to a life of community activism. Julia was studying biology, for lack of a clearer direction, while Rob was immersed in his passion, political science. In his junior year, he was already president of the student senate, and he was working as an intern at a political think tank.

Julia was drawn to his charisma and his passion. Although she considered herself a political agnostic, she admired Rob's causes and was always willing to lend a hand. Rob found Julia attractive for her intelligence and her relaxed, down-to-earth nature. She helped him stay grounded when his passions and energy rose to a frantic level. He, in turn, brought a touch of excitement to her serene world. They thought they were made for each other.

Their relationship was defined by his interests from the start. Their evenings and weekends were filled with political fund-raisers, community meetings, and social events to advance political causes. Rob was finding his way in the world of politics and activism, and he loved the excitement. Julia enjoyed tagging along, and she even began to take a genuine interest. They fell in love quickly, and they were nearly always seen together.

Rob's internship evolved into a job after college, while Julia accepted a materials testing job in a quiet industrial lab. Shortly after graduation, they married and moved to a small bungalow. As before their marriage, Rob's new career filled his nights and weekends with fund-raisers, meetings, and social gatherings. Julia still enjoyed those activities, but she was beginning to see the value of moderation. She wanted to spend time alone with her husband in their new home, perhaps watching a movie or sipping wine in front of the fire. She also began to crave moderation in their conversations. Though she still admired his passion for political causes, she wished they could discuss other topics once in a while.

Julia and Rob became increasingly distant as the first few years of their marriage lumbered by. Her full-time job left her with little energy or desire to accompany him to every function, and so she spent many nights alone.

More than ever, Rob felt he was on a mission with his work, and he couldn't understand why she was withdrawing her support. Though they weren't yet fully aware of it, they had a wide gulf in values that was pushing them apart.

After five years of marriage, their differing values had devolved into disappointment and bitterness. Rob spent increasingly more time with his friends and colleagues in politics, while Julia developed her own circle of friends. They rarely spent evenings or weekends together, and they frequently argued bitterly.

Rob felt abandoned. He had been honest about himself and his lifestyle, and he couldn't understand why Julia no longer participated. In his worst moments, he called her self-centered and cold, and he pressured her to stand by his side as she once did. He despised her friends for, as he saw it, taking her from him. He began drinking in the evenings to dull his sadness.

Julia felt controlled and disrespected. The man who once cherished her now shouted his disapproval. She saw him as narrow-minded and rigid, and she met his complaints with a litany of her own accusations. She even diverged from his political ideology, perhaps out of spite. She disparagingly called him "Rob the Politician," and she called his political views sheeplike and blind. Their insults cut each other to the quick.

Their relationship ended poorly. Their inevitable divorce was legally contentious and expensive. Publicly, they explained their demise by saying they had grown apart. The truth was far worse. These two former lovebirds lost respect for each other. They each left the relationship feeling jaded and filled with animosity.

COOKIE BLINDNESS, AND OTHER SHORTSIGHTED TRICKS OF THE MIND

In retrospect, it's easy to wonder why Rob and Julia got married when their values were so fundamentally different. The answer lies in the powerful urges of the primitive emotional mind's inattentiveness to long-term happiness. Rob and Julia failed to look past their infatuation. Monitoring values is *our* job when the mind has its mind on matters like lust and security.

As we've discussed, the mind's inclinations and sensibilities about potential mates don't extend past the next few hours. Like Rob and Julia, that shortsightedness sets us up for failure.

Our more primitive tastes in romance are similar to other appetites. For instance, we have an instinct to eat cookies, but our instincts don't tell us to stop at one. Cookies are a quick source of energy, and minds like speedy results. Most minds need heavy supervision in the cookie department.

If the mind can't be trusted with cookies, it certainly can't be left unsupervised with a question as consequential as mate choice. Julia's mind was taken by Rob's certainty, his charisma, and his bearing. But as is so often the case, what her mind pursued ultimately became a burden.

With cookies, the mind naturally tends to say *the more, the better.* With mate choice, the mind latches on to surface traits with the same approach: *the more, the better*. Let's look at an example of the manner in which the mind's fixation on surface qualities causes trouble for both genders.

Nice Guys Finish Last, and Other Dirty Tricks of the Mind

In *The Woman's Guide to How Men Think*, I asked men and women for their opinions and peeves about the opposite sex. One of the more common sources of friction between the genders has to do with "nice guys" versus "bad boys." Nice guys routinely complained about women preferring bad boys, and good women frequently complained about nice guys being wimps.

This age-old conflict is a wonderful example of the mind blocking the desires of both genders by drawing our attention toward surface features. It is driven by impulse rather than values.

According to at least one study, there is some truth to men's complaint about women overlooking nice guys. Urbaniak and Kilmann (2006) found women are attracted to men of lower agreeableness for casual flings, preferring physical attractiveness instead. No surprise there, but the researchers found something else. When women are seeking a long-term mate, agreeableness does *not* add to a man's chances of success. It may actually work against him.

The researchers were examining "agreeable" guys rather than the more loosely defined "nice" guys. Agreeableness is one of the big five personality traits that serve as well-defined, commonly accepted constructs researchers can easily measure. (The others are openness, conscientiousness, extraversion, and neuroticism.) A person who scores high in agreeableness is trusting, straightforward, altruistic, compliant, and tender-minded (Costa and Mc-Crae 1992).

From an evolutionary standpoint, a woman's mind might not appreciate those "nice" qualities in a potential mate. Her mind may find them downright unappealing, and for good reason. When we scan potential mates, our minds make snap judgments about who might make an ideal partner. Women and men both measure a few surface characteristics, and anyone who doesn't clear the first hurdle will find it hard to win our affection. (I'm sure this is nothing new. Overcoming the first cut in the draft picks of love is fodder for any number of Hugh Grant movies.)

Our minds do this automatically, creating a pool of eligible mates who look great on the outside—some of them like old clunkers with new paint jobs. We wouldn't want anyone we care about to make decisions in such a shortsighted manner, but we're all predisposed to it.

In a classic study, Buss and Barnes (1986) found physical attractiveness to be one of the first qualities men look for in women. (Sometimes researchers begin by confirming what seems patently obvious.) Women, in contrast, default to men who appear to have solid earning capacity. These are the most basic surface features that draw us in.

Of course, those aren't the only considerations. Both genders reported a need for qualities like kindness, understanding, and intelligence, but both genders also possessed hasty minds with shortsighted tastes. However, I don't believe that indicates shallowness in either gender. Quite the contrary, I think.

Though Buss and Barnes didn't say so, high-earning capacity is a proxy for larger character traits our female ancestors would have found necessary and attractive. Women long ago would have needed a man who could provide safety, provisions, and social standing while she was effectively immobilized by pregnancy and child rearing. She would have wanted the kind of stand-up Cro-Magnon who was strong enough to help slay dangerous beasts, assertive enough to claim his share for the family, and charismatic enough to maintain dependable relationships with the rest of the clan.

Today, a man with high earning capacity is similarly likely to be a man whose character is forceful enough to thrive in a competitive social environment. Research has shown that men who are highly agreeable make less money and are less frequently considered for advancement than men of low agreeableness (Judge, Livingston, and Hurst 2012). Life may be more comfortable today than it was for our ancestors, but little has changed in the social environment. Men still need to be assertive if they are to succeed.

A smart woman's mind is attuned to these social necessities and steers her toward mates who it *thinks* will be assets rather than a burden—and hence the mind's attention and attraction to surface characteristics that reflect solid earning capacity. You can't blame a mind for looking out for its owner.

There's a downside to the mind's blindness to subtleties. A man doesn't need to be a disagreeable jerk in order to be assertive, but the shortsighted mind can easily overlook that muted truth. To some degree, high-earning capacity is a reflection of assertiveness, and just as with cookies, the mind tends to err on the side of overkill: *If a little assertiveness is good, then a lot must be better.* This is just one example of humanity's blunt predisposition to seek mates who might be hellish in the long run.

Getting back to the men who have complained about women who reject nice guys, I wonder if those men are displaying an overly compromising nature, which might suggest they are unwilling to defend what matters. Passiveness in a man would have been repellent to our female ancestors, and women today have probably inherited some measure of that sensibility.

I think it's us men, not women, who create a false dilemma. We complain that either we can be nice and we'll be lonely, or we can be jerks and the ladies will dig us. Some men understandably but misguidedly believe they must pick a side, naughty or nice. People do tend to see the world in black and white, after all.

Maybe the third option for men is to strike a balance between sensitivity and assertiveness, and for women to seek that wise balance in their choice of partner.

Wise couples seek precisely that sort of balance in a partner. Julia might have done well to seek someone who was passionately involved in community since she found that quality attractive, but who was also occasionally willing to tune out his passions in exchange for intimacy. Instead, she followed her mind into the "more is better" trap only to discover that there can be too much charisma and leadership in a man.

Julia's dilemma is probably as old as humanity. It's an example of inborn predilections men and women unknowingly carry, and so both genders can be ensnared in this false dichotomy. It is also an example of our minds compelling us to make choices based on short-term considerations that may fail in the long run.

Consider the mind's romantic attraction to narcissistic individuals. Narcissists have difficulty maintaining relationships due to a deficit in their ability to tend the needs and desires of others. They have a grandiose sense of importance, they are preoccupied with fantasies of their own brilliance, beauty, and success. They tend to believe they are entitled to special treatment and obedience. They can be exploitative, arrogant, and unfeeling (American Psychiatric Association 2013).

There's no denying those are poor qualities in a partner, yet research has shown that men and women both judge narcissists of the opposite sex to be more attractive than nonnarcissists (Dufner et al. 2013). Perhaps it's because narcissists put more effort into their first impressions and their physical appeal. They make a bold and positive first impression. They appear confident, and they like themselves.

Here's the intriguing discovery. The researchers found that even though we regard narcissists as potential mates, we *don't* regard them as adequate friend material. We see right through them— right up to the moment we're looking for love, when our minds are particularly prone to addled, short-term decision making.

What we *say* we look for in a mate and what we *actually* are drawn to can be entirely different. When it comes to long-term

happiness, sometimes our minds are hopelessly daft. Thank goodness for the compass offered by well-defined values. We'll discuss
how to define them shortly. But first, a few words about happy
couples and shared values.

What Happy Couples Look Like

We don't need to exclude those shiny surface features entirely.
Lust is fun, and being in the company of people who awaken the
animal in us is one of life's joys. But the charm of animal mag-
netism wears off quickly when we desire deeper connection. Here
are some factors to consider as you think about shared values.

Excitement vs. calmness. Some people like curling up
on the couch with a movie; others prefer motorcycles and
rock climbing. The first style of activity reflects a desire to
experience calmness, relaxation, and peace. Researchers
call it the *affiliative motive*. The second, called *power motive*,
reflects a desire to feel strong, excited, and enthusiastic.

Couples are more satisfied when they have similar
preferences for excitement or calmness (Job, Bernecker,
and Dweck 2012). Couples who share a common predi-
lection tend to create feelings of satisfaction by spending
time together in mutually satisfying activities.

Common goals. People are happier, and emotional
well-being is higher, when goals and values are congruent.
On the other hand, happiness and well-being are lower
when we see ourselves pursuing goals incompatible with
our values. For example, people who value family and
intimacy sacrifice happiness when they exchange those
activities for financial and career achievement (Brunstein,
Schultheiss, and Grässmann 1998).

It's easier to pursue values-congruent goals when a
partner shares or at least supports those values. This was
the downfall of Julia's relationship. As her values matured,

she and Rob discovered their incompatibilities, and each was forced to relinquish a portion of their individual goals or else pursue them under the disapproval of their mate. Those are lousy options.

Desire for closeness. Couples who have similar desires for emotional connectedness report higher relationship satisfaction. Incongruent desires in this area contribute to risk of breakup (Hagemeyer et al. 2012). In other words, couples who share similar relationship values for closeness have similar levels of satisfaction. The higher their shared desire for closeness, the easier it is to reach their goals and the more satisfied each partner is.

Quality of shared time. Spending lots of time together doesn't necessarily lead to relationship satisfaction. Togetherness can even lead to dissatisfaction and boredom if it isn't meaningful. Merely enjoying your partner's company isn't enough in the long run. Sharing activities you each find stimulating directly improves relationship satisfaction (Reissman, Aron, and Bergen 1993).

Perceived similarity vs. shared values. We feel better about ourself, our partner, and our relationship if we perceive our partner to be similar to us, but sometimes the perception of similarity is erroneous. People tend to project their own relationship-relevant traits onto others to whom they're attracted, imagining similarities that may not exist. The more attracted we are to a person, the more we project ourselves onto our partner (Morry, Kito, and Ortiz 2011). We're also more tolerant of perceived differences if we feel safe in the relationship. Focusing on positive events and remembering the good times helps to increase the perception of similarity.

This has a couple of implications for relationships.

First, it's natural to fool ourselves into seeing shared values when we have the hots for someone. Second, wide gulfs can develop in relationships when people lose sight of their similarities. People grow and change throughout the course of a relationship. Focusing on commonalities helps maintain attraction and satisfaction.

Common desires for excitement or calmness, similar goals, meaningful shared activities, and perceptions of closeness—these connections keep couples happy long after infatuation wears off.

Defining Your Values

The mind is not the enemy—it just needs a little help with long-term decisions. Clearly defined values might be your most reliable insurance against a big relationship mistake like the one Julia and Rob made.

Values become clearer when we think of them not as attributes but as behavior. Values are what we *do*. Though it's essential to understand what kind of person we'd like to meet, it's just as important to know what kind of person we want to *be* in a relationship. What's your ideal self? How do you want others to think of you?

Let's look at a couple of ways to think about values, starting with a philosophical approach suitable for candlelight dinner conversations or good-natured kitchen debates, and then a more nuts-and-bolts approach for day-to-day application.

First, the airy, philosophical approach—or maybe it's more sociological. In either case, Shalom Schwartz (2012) has identified what he believes to be ten universal value categories that apply across cultures. In an extensive study, he narrowed the most commonly endorsed human concerns to ten categories. How would you rate the importance of each of these in your life?

- Self-direction: self-reliance and independent thought
- Stimulation: variety, adventure, and risk taking
- Hedonism: gratification and comfort

- Achievement: personal success and competence
- Power: social status and prestige; dominance over people and resources
- Security: safety and harmony in society, relationships, and self
- Conformity: compliance and self-restraint; placing the group's needs above those of the individual
- Tradition: customs handed down by family, culture, or religion
- Benevolence: loyalty and caring for friends and family
- Universalism: understanding others and providing equal treatment for different people and groups

Schwartz's list should provide plenty of conversational fodder for you and that special guy you're getting to know. It's also a bit lofty. What about the more day-to-day application of values? Here's another way to think about them adapted from the world of behavioral psychology (Dahl et al. 2009). You might keep a couple of questions in mind as you read them: how important is each category to you, and what behaviors do you associate with it? (Here's another opportunity to record your thoughts in a journal. These questions are important, so take your time. I'll wait. I've also put some guidelines after the questions to help you start.)

- Career: What kind of work do you find valuable? What kind of person do you want to be in your work?
- Leisure activity: What activities do you find relaxing or rejuvenating? What hobbies bring you joy?
- Caregiving: How important is it for you to care for and inspire others?
- Family: What type of sister, mother, daughter do you want to be? What sorts of relationships do you want to build with your immediate family? Your extended family? Your in-laws?

- Intimate relationships: What kind of partner do you want to be? What kind of relationship would you like to build? Who is the ideal *you* in your relationship?
- Community involvement: Would you like to contribute to political, social, environmental, or other community causes? What kind of position do you wish to occupy within your community?
- Religion and spirituality: What form of spirituality, if any, matters to you? What role do you want religion or spirituality to play in your life? How would you describe your ideal self in regard to your spirituality?
- Education and personal development: What education or skills do you most value? How important is ongoing education, and what role do you want it to play in your life?
- Health: How do you approach mental and physical fitness? What kind of relationship do you wish to have with food, exercise, sleep, substances, and intellectual pursuits?
- Friends: What qualities do you want to bring to your friendships? What kinds of friendships do you want to build?
- Other: What is missing from this list that is vital to a meaningful life? How do you want to enact this value in your life?

I'll add two more items that didn't make the cut in the behavioral literature, but are some of the biggest sources of closeness and conflict in romantic relationships:

- Finances: What does money represent to you? Freedom? Security? Something different? How do you balance future security against current enjoyment? How do you want to approach bills, debts, and financial obligations?
- Physical intimacy: What are your preferences and sensibilities regarding physical intimacy and sex in a relationship? How important are sex and other physical expressions of affection? How do you want physical intimacy to figure into your relationship?

Some people assign a 1–10 score for each value category to reflect its importance. Maybe community involvement doesn't matter at all, so it gets a zero, but you live for your friendships, so that category gets a 10. Another strategy is to remove half of the less important categories, and then half again, to pare the list down to what *really* matters. Don't worry if you struggle with these questions. Most people do. Here are some tips to help you define your values.

Be specific. If you have trouble knowing which of these value categories matter most, you might list the behaviors you associate with them. For example, the behaviors you associate with family might include organizing birthday parties, maintaining the family history and family tree, and being the best parent you can be. A values-driven life is in the details.

Check your rearview mirror. Looking back on your life can uncover your most treasured values. A young client of mine had trouble identifying what she cherished. Her values became clearer when she looked back on the most meaningful times and realized how prominent children had been. She had worked as a babysitter at every opportunity, she treasured the moments she got to spend with her nephews, and she had coached children at youth camps. That retrospective helped her decide where she wanted to take her profession and her relationships.

Explore the ideal world. What would you do with your life if money were no object? If no one was watching? If no one was judging or rewarding you? You might also think about what would hurt most if it were missing from your life.

Separate goals from values. Goals come and go. You achieve one goal, and then you set another. But values are never complete. No matter how consistently you pursue your values, you can always take one more step. For example, you might have a goal of earning more money this year. That doesn't necessarily mean "career" is one of your prime values because "earning more money" might not describe the kind of person you want to be in your career.

Get comfortable with the discomfort of values. Living a values-driven existence is bound to get uncomfortable. We'll eventually be forced to defend our values or make an onerous choice because of them. Suppose you feel compelled to leave an employer because the company's values collide with yours, or you must choose to forgo fun activities or potential romantic relationships when they clash with your values. How do you want to act in these situations? You'll truly know your values when life makes it uncomfortable to live in the service of them.

The perfect man doesn't necessarily possess values that flawlessly match yours. Variety is fun, and separate interests are healthy. Problems arise mainly when values collide, as they did with Rob and Julia. We can apply our two values models—the philosophical and the practical—to describe their differences.

Using Schwartz's philosophical list, Rob's higher-order values included power, achievement, conformity, and stimulation. Julia's values, which she didn't identify until later in the relationship, included security, benevolence, and gratification. They were quite different from Rob's.

Using the nuts-and-bolts list from behavioral psychology, Rob's values were narrowly focused on community involvement and career. There's nothing wrong with a narrow focus. Concentration is a source of mastery. The only snag was its incompatibility with Julia's values. She wanted to focus on family, caring for others, and enjoying time with friends. They struck out on this list, too. Rob and Julia might have realized their lives were on perilously different trajectories had they taken time to discuss and clarify values early in the relationship.

Dodging Values Traps

Rob and Julia's mistake was a case of simple neglect. They were so enamored with each other, and so enthralled with the excitement of Rob's life, they failed to examine the basic question of compatibility before building a life together.

Values are easy to neglect, especially when they're eclipsed by the intoxicating feeling of a new love (or the oppressed feeling of an old, unhealthy love). We can easily drift away from a values-driven life if we're not careful. Here are three "values traps" adapted from Dahl et al. (2009). They can leave us with a life we had no intention of living.

Avoiding unpleasant thoughts and feelings. Living in the service of our values isn't easy. The more meaningful a thing is to us, the greater the risk that we will one day suffer disappointment or loss. That ugly little fact of life compels us to protect our cherished thing and avoid the pain it might one day bring. The fear of loss and pain sometimes keeps people in broken-down relationships, compelling them to sacrifice their values. Or, as we saw with Colleen in chapter 2, the fear of loss and pain can keep us from pursuing what we want.

Pursuing secondary rewards such as admiration or security. Money, position, admiration—these are fun, but they also come with the risk of veering us away from our cherished values. Being the best student, or mother, or CEO you can be doesn't always come with accolades. Likewise, the best relationships don't necessarily bring financial security or adoring approval from friends and family.

On the other hand, romantic relationships that are based on secondary rewards like money and adventure aren't always the healthiest. Either way, the bill always comes due when we place secondary rewards before values.

Keeping up appearances. Sometimes we allow others' expectations to eclipse our values, especially those of us motivated to make others happy through self-sacrifice. It's a great example of the kind of double bind our values can create. Remaining in a relationship for the approval of friends and family is like refusing to sell a lemon of a car because you don't want to hurt your mechanic's feelings. It becomes a burden and an encumbrance to a values-driven life.

Please don't feel guilty if you find yourself getting off track with values. Acting inconsistently with our values is probably more normal than we'd like to think. Values require diligence.

Sacrificing your values for a relationship usually has warning signs. You might notice yourself making excuses for what you would normally consider obnoxious behavior in your partner. You might hear your friends and family say things such as "that's not like you." Or you might simply have a queasy feeling about your decisions.

Julia's story shows that sometimes love isn't enough, no matter what you may have heard from Shakespeare and Lord Byron. Opposing values can be titillating in the beginning of a relationship. They take a toll when the passion fades.

Opposing values, however, aren't bound to be disastrous. Couples do learn to live with different values. It can even be a point of pride to succeed despite your differences—one partner being a vegan, atheistic liberal, and the other a meat-eating, God-fearing conservative. I've seen couples enjoy their differences. It requires excellent problem-solving, communication, and compromise skills. All I ask is that you avoid entering any relationship blind to one of the most prominent factors in long-term relationship success.

What If You're Already Committed but Your Values Collide?

Differing values can be wonderful. Maybe he values working on cars (under the headings of education and leisure) and she values karate classes (health and community), and they support each other's activities, even if they don't quite understand the appeal. It's a great source of closeness when couples can support each other's activities.

We're often drawn to people who complement and balance our predisposition. For example, a party animal might be drawn to someone who is more sedate, and vice versa. Couples with differing inclinations can bring balance to each other. But relationships take extra work when those differences rise to the level of moral or spiritual dissimilarity.

Sometimes couples choose to slog through opposing values, as when trying to repair a relationship for the sake of children. Here are a few tips to help navigate differences in the event you're already committed to someone whose values are distant from your own.

> **Embrace the other side of the coin.** The qualities we are drawn to in a partner frequently turn out to annoy us down the road. The party animal who marries the homebody might appreciate the sanity he or she brings, but eventually the party animal becomes terribly annoyed when the homebody wants to leave the office holiday party early in the evening. In those moments, it helps to remember that the qualities we find most vexing are often the other side of a quality we once found endearing.

Agree to disagree. Respect your differences. Remind each other that differing values (or complementary values, if you want a more positive spin) are part of the reason you chose each other. Agree to allow each other the time and space to pursue valued activities. Catch yourselves and agree to disagree at the first sign you're reviving an old, futile argument. Sometimes it helps to completely disengage with each other and go to separate locations until passions subside.

Talk about it, up to the point of diminishing returns. Don't let your differences fester. Opposing values hold the seeds of contempt, and contempt is ruinous to relationships. Know when to end the conversation and agree to disagree. Not every conversation needs to have a tidy resolution. Good people can disagree, and there is wisdom in allowing differences to exist.

Find your common ground. Avoid becoming so fixated on your differences that you lose sight of your common interests. Seek the balance between individual activities and those that bring meaning to you both.

Finally, if you find you cannot pursue your values without harsh judgment or rejection, then the relationship may be in need of repair. A few hours invested with a skillful relationship psychologist can pay off handsomely by reestablishing healthy communication patterns and mutual respect.

Taking Your History, Patterns, and Values on the Road of Love

Clearly defined values give us the motivation and the means to lovingly disobey our demanding, emotional, shortsighted minds. "Disobey" is the key word. Disobedience frees us from the shackles of the past. Our minds are only looking out for us, so there's no need to beat them up or torture ourselves trying to conquer them. We can simply say to our minds: *no, thanks.*

We can pack it all up and take it with us on the road of love—the relationship history, the core beliefs (both useful and otherwise), the relationship patterns we have inherited and built upon, and our all-important values.

We are taught to seek what we're attracted to in romance, making goodness-of-fit a secondary consideration. That approach can create precisely the kind of relationships we *don't* want. Turning that formula on its head is the recipe for success. The most beautiful and lasting relationships exist within the realm of good fit.

As we go forward, I hope you will carry lightly your history, your beliefs, and your patterns. Let your heart be your advisor, but let values be your compass.

Now let's turn our attention to the good men of the world.

Part II
Three Pillars
of a Good Man

Love isn't always enough. Happy relationships start with good raw material.

You wouldn't hire an accountant who doesn't own a calculator, or a carpenter who has no tools. They'll waste your time and leave a mess for you to clean up. Every job requires proper tools and solid skills. The same is true of relationships.

Relationship-ready men possess three fundamental traits:

- sense of purpose
- good mental health
- emotional maturity

These are the "three pillars" of a good man. Think of them as the minimum requirements for any man who hopes to earn your love.

CHAPTER 4
SENSE OF PURPOSE

What makes a man ready for a serious relationship? It begins with a sense of purpose and the striving for fulfillment in life.

A sense of purpose is one of the most basic needs of any happy and healthy man, and it's harder for men to succeed in relationships without it. In this chapter, we'll look at three central features of a man's sense of purpose:

- status
- responsibility
- a sense of effectiveness

Romance suffers when men are unfulfilled in their sense of purpose. Need an example? Look no further than Aaron.

BRIDGET AND AARON: LIVING WITH A RUDDERLESS MAN

Bridget felt as if she were on a relationship teeter-totter with Aaron. Things seemed great one day and hopeless the next.

Anyone would have told you Aaron was a great guy. People liked his quick wit and his energy. He easily impressed people with his personality. But he had always struggled to maintain jobs and steady relationships. He was still floundering as he approached thirty-four and had been dating Bridget for nearly two years.

Mostly aimless in his ambitions, Aaron would wander from job to job. Every few months he would develop a new professional ambition, most of which amounted to little more than grandiose goals for quick wealth. He would immerse himself in the idea of opening a coin-op car wash, or writing a book, or even becoming some sort of business consultant. His passion would fade as reality set in. He would sink into discouragement and withdraw from Bridget.

Bridget recognized the cycle but didn't know what to do about it. She didn't care where he worked. She simply wanted him to be happy and for the two of them to build a life together. He would still speak to her during his discouraged phases and try to create hope for their future together, but Bridget found him to be emotionally absent, losing himself in pot and video games. Although Bridget and Aaron spoke of marriage and children, she had stark concerns about his ability to function as a husband and father with these wild swings in self-image.

Aaron's lack of focus and follow-through weren't surprising in light of his early experiences. Although he had been a bright and energetic child, he earned mostly Cs in school, thanks to the same type of daydreaming that hindered him as an adult. His father was disengaged and created no expectations or structure. His mother was a driven career woman who surfaced periodically in Aaron's life to offer disapproval, but little guidance. More often than not his parents were distracted by their own ongoing marital conflict.

Aaron had taken up no goals or interests as a child. Instead, he relied on his ability to charm and entertain people. Perhaps his teachers and family failed to notice his academic struggles because they were dazzled by his wonderfully effective social skills.

Some kids require little guidance; others, like Aaron, require a great deal. Sadly, he was deprived of it. He felt lost by the time he graduated high school. He had no idea how to identify a meaningful goal, let alone stick to it. He took whatever work came his way, always wishing he had something more.

He was painfully aware of his aimlessness, and he avoided thinking about it by distracting himself with his social life, marijuana, and video games. Gaming offered trivial goals to pursue, and he derived just enough challenge and purpose from his jobs to keep him psychologically afloat. When he was feeling upbeat he would latch on to big dreams he had no idea how to pursue, then eventually he would sink again into sadness.

Now, as an adult, he was going nowhere. He hadn't been prepared for manhood. He was in no condition to become a husband and father. He could learn the skills, but it might take years to make up for lost time. In the best-case scenario, Aaron would begin learning discipline, focus, and devotion in his mid-thirties (better late than never). In the worst-case scenario, he might flounder for the rest of his life.

Bridget knew what she wanted in a relationship: steadiness, happiness, and children. She would have to decide whether to spend her valuable time hoping and waiting for Aaron to find his way.

Why a Man Card Makes Him a Better Partner

Selflessness is a special part of the male psyche. It's as old as humanity, and it is a prime component in the proverbial "man card." While human conditions have changed from the time when men gave of themselves by risking their lives on the hunting grounds, what's come to be called a man card still helps men succeed in relationships. Aaron was a nice and attractive guy, but did he possess a man card?

If you'll permit me, I'll define a *man card* as the intangible certification that causes the community to respect a man. Community expectations, and the male psyche that strives to satisfy them, have been shaped by a lot of history.

If there's one single measure of a man card, it's the expectation that the man produce more than he consumes. At least, that's the conclusion drawn by social psychologist Roy Baumeister (2010), who has examined societies both ancient and modern. Dr. Baumeister wrote: "If the culture can convince most or all of the men to produce more than they consume, then the culture will be rich. It will have a surplus, at least, that it can use to take care of many who cannot care for themselves, including the children, the elderly, the sick and injured" (197).

In other words, when Prehistoric Pete went hunting, it would have been bad form to return home with only enough to feed himself. He would have been shamed for it. He was expected to return home with bounty enough to feed the clan, and he was expected to risk his life doing so, if necessary. His reward was praise, respect, and admiration. His reward was his man card.

This ancient, cross-cultural expectation has profoundly shaped the modern male mind. It's the mental baggage we men carry. It's one of the many gender-based motivations that made perfect sense to our ancestors. Evolutionary psychologists argue that humanity would not have survived without the gender-based division of labor that gave rise to male openhandedness.

Those ancient motivations echo strongly in the modern mind, even if environments and societies have changed. I think it's the reason men today compete for the privilege of picking up the check at restaurants. Good men feel compelled to provide, and we want a little taste of Prehistoric Pete's glory.

Beyond those evolutionary considerations, a giving heart is a wonderful quality in a partner, male or female. Historic gender roles and sensibilities might be unappealing to the modern ear in some quarters, but the appeal of partners who are willing and able to contribute more than they consume should be a no-brainer.

Here's an ancient parable I just made up. There was once a woman who received two wedding proposals. One man was a laborer who, hoping to win the woman's heart, saved his earnings for many months in order to provide a modest but sweet wedding. The other was a wealthy man of leisure who, assuming his financial standing was irresistible, insisted she pay half the marriage expenses. She chose the poor laborer because a man's ability to be generous and devoted means nothing if he lacks the willingness to do so.

This ancient male drive to provide isn't as anachronistic as it may seem. The desire to provide more than one consumes—be it materially, emotionally, or otherwise—is a critical characteristic in any partner. While researchers have focused on the male drive to be a provider, generosity as a personal characteristic helps both genders succeed in relationships. Consider the alternative partner: one who looks out for himself at your expense.

Far from being outdated, generosity is one measure of a man's ability to devote himself and his willingness to be a fully functioning partner. My contrived little parable fits what wise women have told me about successful relationships. I conducted a survey while writing this book, asking both men and women what makes for a good man. On the matter of resources, not a single woman told me their man needs to be wealthy. Instead, they said a good man is *willing* to care for others. Here are a few of their comments

> *"A good man is a caretaker, meaning someone whose life is devoted to caring for others. He not only provides materially for his loved ones, but tends to their emotional and, in the case of his children, educational needs. He lives for others."*

> *"A good man is strong for his family."*

> *"One who has a sincere, unselfish desire to help you, please you, and cherish you—not to get anything in return, but because he feels it's the right way to be."*

"A good man is someone who cares about others and puts his family and loved ones first. Someone who gives without expecting something in return."

The men who answered my survey were in agreement.

"A good man is the person who goes above and beyond to help his friends and family and is willing to compromise his own well-being to provide for them. The key is that this person should do this without need for congratulations, and will even do the right thing when no one is watching."

"A good man takes care of himself and others."

"Good men are providers, protectors, and good role models for young males."

"A good man knows his value without being arrogant."

That last one is particularly important to relationships: "A good man knows his value."

Lack of purpose (or "value") is a terrible malady to the male mind. In the worst cases, it contributes to the downfall of young men, leading them toward unhealthy and desperate bids for purpose like joining street gangs or engaging in risky behavior. Or it leads them to numb their sense of aimlessness with substance abuse or other damaging behavior.

In milder cases, it leads to the kind of disengaged melancholy and ineffectualness that dogged Aaron. When purpose is gone, so is a sense of masculinity, and sometimes even a man's reason for being. Here's what one man told me about knowing his purpose, and how women sometimes don't understand the way it drives men: "I think women have a hard time understanding what drives men to work as hard as we do. My motivation is a yearning to leave a legacy" (S. T. Smith 2013, 19).

If I've given the impression that the need to be useful is a burden for most men, it isn't. Dutifulness makes most men feel alive.

Clearly, having a sense of purpose mattered to Aaron, and that's why its absence hurt so much. But it isn't equally important to all men. Some men reject the notion of a man card and choose *not* to be of service to others.

These men aren't missing a piece of their soul; they're simply choosing a different path. I don't believe they deserve a moment's criticism. At the same time, anyone who is unmotivated to look beyond their own interests is unlikely to be happy or successful in long-term, loving relationships.

If that assumption is true, then the woman in my contrived parable made the wise choice. The poor man was purposeful and selfless. Sooner or later, every couple faces hardship, and it's always handier to face life's challenges with one's man card intact.

How can you tell if a man is maintaining his man card? By exploring his beliefs about three lynchpins of respectable male community:

- status
- responsibility
- effectiveness

Status

Status in this case doesn't mean achievement, as in "that guy sure attained high status when his company's IPO netted him three million dollars." *Status*, in our discussion, simply refers to a man's social standing. It's his rank, if you will, among his peers and colleagues.

High achievement is a different matter entirely. Some men who are the best boyfriend or husband material are utterly unconcerned with power or riches. And, as various philandering CEOs and elected officials have shown time and again, sometimes the man with high social rank makes a terrible partner. Ambition matters less in romance than a clear sense of status, and a man of purpose knows where he stands in relation to other people.

I have heard many women say they don't understand men's preoccupation with status. "Preoccupation" may not be too strong a word to describe the male proclivity to monitor rank and status.

We men possess special cognitive skills for assessing our position in the pack. We can switch roles and status almost effortlessly, we can establish leadership roles quickly and without violence, and, thanks to our deference to status, we are highly cooperative in groups. Men are more cooperative than women in some contexts, and we routinely monitor our status and recalibrate our assumptions about position (S. T. Smith 2013).

A confident and assured man can speak comfortably about his position among other men. He knows who's the expert, who's the boss, who's responsible for the grunt work, and he's aware of every significant status change within his work or social group. He's comfortable being both mentor and student, and if he holds a sense of resentment or entitlement about his status, he keeps it to himself unless he's ready to assume responsibility and take charge.

A man's sense of status is part of his sense of purpose, and a barometer of how connected and attentive he is to others. It's a reflection of his relationships skills, and it shows in his words and his deeds.

A man is missing a critical compass when he miscalculates his place among others, or when he has no place among others thanks to a lack of involvement. Aaron, nice guy though he was, had a great deal of growth ahead of him. His sense of status wavered dramatically from one day to the next, as his dreams waxed and waned.

The status he imagined rarely matched his reality. At any given moment he was either over- or underestimating his place among others. He had no overriding purpose by which to accurately gauge his place in society, and so his self-concept was at the whim of mood and circumstance.

Responsibility, or commitment to others, is another indication that a good man has a sense of purpose. Like high social status, a good man doesn't necessarily seek out copious responsibilities. We can't all be generals or neurosurgeons, nor do we need to be. But a purposeful man welcomes the commitment to something larger than himself.

That allegiance could be to family, coworkers, the church, the military, or a group of community activists, just to name a few possibilities. Placing effort and focus toward his commitment to others indicates he is a man of purpose and dedication. He's better suited to relationships than the man who lacks these abilities.

Men need responsibility. It makes us healthy. It has been well-documented that men die sooner than women in all age groups, partly because we are less likely to maintain our physical health, eat and sleep well, wear seat belts, or have a large support group. We are also more likely to smoke, become alcoholics, and engage in criminal activity (Garfield, Isacco, and Bartlo 2010).

Those counterproductive habits change when a man takes on responsibility. Garfield and colleagues found that three-quarters of the men they interviewed reported positive changes to their health behaviors when they chose to embrace a responsibility such as fatherhood. Once men embraced meaningful responsibilities, their diets improved, they exercised more, drank less, reduced their risk-taking behavior, and took better care of themselves in general. One man even reported eating more vegetables. Responsibility changes a man in ways that can literally extend his life.

Responsibility was also missing from Aaron's life. He had lacked the ability to stay focused long enough for people to put him in a position of trust. He held jobs in which he could be easily replaced, and therefore he had no teammates to depend on him for anything more than punching in on time.

Aaron had not earned a position of responsibility among his family either. And as for his role among friends, he served no purpose larger than playing video games with them. He certainly hadn't earned Bridget's trust as a dependable figure in her life. No one depended on Aaron. He was essentially a man of leisure, and it ate at his soul.

My intent is not to beat up on Aaron. He was suffering enough as it was. But Bridget would be wise to take note of his lack of focus and determination before committing a lifetime to him.

Effectiveness

There's another bit of cultural compulsion that has been handed down through countless generations of men: the need to be talented and effective. This is no mere, boring sociological lecture. OK, well maybe a bit, but there's a reason for it. A man's sense of effectiveness has a deep influence on his romantic fitness.

In cultures the world over, and throughout recorded history, men have been judged by achievements, and boys have had to prove their worthiness. Before they could be called men, boys of most cultures, some still in existence, had to withstand pain, hunt a dangerous animal, or master an arduous task. Tests of manhood involve overcoming stiff odds, and boys aren't considered men until they succeed.

Here in Western society, men are still judged on achievement, even though we've mostly relinquished dangerous and painful rites of passage. Two American researchers have found the male rite of passage continues, even if in a different form: "Compared with womanhood, which is typically viewed as resulting from a natural, permanent, and biological developmental transition, manhood must be earned and maintained through publicly verifiable actions" (Vandello and Bosson 2013, 101).

Proof of manhood in modern Western society might come from professional, academic, or military success. Luckily, we don't generally need to subject ourselves to painful rituals—subcultures like gangs and fraternities notwithstanding—but the requirement exists nonetheless. Young American men *and* women attribute "womanhood" to a physical maturity, while they attribute "manhood" to hard-won social achievements that must be actively and repeatedly demonstrated.

The same researchers also found the "elusive" and "tenuous" nature of manhood is no small source of stress for men (Bosson and Vandello 2011). Men whose man cards (my term, not theirs) are threatened through shame or humiliation usually feel compelled to defend their reputations.

The more anxiety and conflict a man feels around his hard-to-earn, easy-to-lose masculinity, the likelier he is to experience lower well-being, greater depression, substance abuse and risky behaviors, and a lower likelihood of seeking help (O'Neil 2008). Lost masculinity is a formidable obstacle for men to overcome.

Some people might find such rigid gender roles to be distasteful; others think they serve an ancient and noble purpose. I won't advance either agenda on these pages. Whether or not we like the notion of the man card and its effect on male mental health, it just *is*. A man who questions his masculinity is going to struggle in life and in relationships.

This was yet another deficit chipping away at Aaron's relationship fitness. He hadn't demonstrated effectiveness in the world. He had no skills or accomplishments on which to hang his hat. At his late age, he still hadn't passed society's test and earned his man card. He surely felt that deficit deep in his soul.

A man needs to be skilled at something. Expertise is good for his mental health, and it's expected of him. He doesn't need to change the world; he simply needs something on which to claim manhood. He needs to know he has made the world a slightly better place.

THE PRICE OF PURPOSE

A man's sense of purpose matters because when status, responsibility, and effectiveness are absent, then frustration and emptiness take their place. A man without a sense of purpose might still be a decent guy, like Aaron, and he might even be worth pursuing, but his relationship engine probably won't be firing on all cylinders. Fortunately, it is never too late for men like Aaron.

Everything in life comes with trade-offs, and a man's sense of purpose is no exception. Purpose often comes with both ambition and a sense of duty—two male qualities that can be simultaneously attractive and vexing for women. A man's sense of purpose necessarily divides his attention. It sometimes creates split allegiances and distraction from his romantic relationship.

In *The Woman's Guide to How Men Think*, I told the story of Sam and Tamara. Sam was a good man who was torn between the devotion he felt for his wife and family, and the duty and ambition he felt for his workplace.

Those split allegiances nearly cost him his marriage because neither he nor Tamara realized the nature of his struggle. He felt torn because Tamara was exhausted and needed his help at home, while at the same time his company was demanding more of his time and attention.

Sam relied on his male social calculus to solve the problem. Since he felt he had to choose, he reckoned the family could survive an angry Tamara more easily than they could survive a downgrade in income. Ancient male logic led him to work harder and provide more resources. Ironically, his decision increased the problems at home.

It never occurred to Sam to simply speak to Tamara about his bind rather than solving the problem on his own. Luckily, Sam and Tamara eventually talked and found a more ideal solution.

Sam's story illustrates the kind of double bind men frequently find themselves in. If they devote more time to the family, they could lose standing on the team. That can have serious ramifications. If they give more time to the team, people at home will be unhappy. Their natural inclination, thanks to eons of evolution, may be to defer to the team. There's a reason for it.

Evolutionary psychologist Mark Van Vugt (2007) believes the countless violent conflicts waged between small groups of our distant ancestors has left a deep need for group allegiance on the male mind. On the whole, men are more group oriented than women, and men are more altruistically committed to their group than women during times of intergroup competition. Van Vugt suggests that evolutionary forces have bred men to be highly attuned to the needs of their team and highly willing to pitch in during times of conflict or competition.

As a young child, I frequently visited the small Kansas town of Ness City. Small towns need fire departments just like big towns, but they lack the funding to support a staff of paid firefighters.

Instead, they build centrally located buildings housing fire engines and other equipment, and the volunteer staff live off-site. When there's an emergency, an alarm goes out to those volunteers. They stop whatever they're doing—even family time—and race to the firehouse.

I recall desperately wanting to be a volunteer firefighter. I dreamed of answering the call when the community was in need. I experienced that urge before I could recite my times tables. Admittedly, I was slow to learn my times tables, but I'm sure you get my point. It was a strangely powerful urge for a young boy, and it's a common one. Van Vugt's observations suggest that the instinct to support the team is deeply ingrained in the male psyche.

Men of purpose face a challenge. It's our job to discuss our responsibilities with our loved ones, and to establish balance between our professional and personal allegiances.

Male purpose also presents a challenge for women. Though the man of purpose is better equipped for a relationship than the rudderless man, he will feel compelled at times to take time away from the relationship to work on maintaining his man card. Society demands his time and energy. But the longer we're away with the team, the more we yearn to come home. It's a wise woman who realizes a man will return from duty eager to embrace his most important relationship.

CHAPTER 5
GOOD MENTAL HEALTH

I have heard thoughtful, intelligent people suggest that men don't experience emotions as deeply as women. It's an easy conclusion to draw, but the idea that men and women possess fundamentally different emotional capacities doesn't quite add up. We're of the same species. Our brains have the same basic structure. We may have quantifiably *different* emotional experiences, but I'm aware of no evidence that men possess *fewer* emotions. To the contrary, I've seen enough bar fights and broken-hearted gents to know that male emotions run deep.

The illusion that men experience fewer emotions leads some mental-health professionals to believe men have fewer emotional problems. That belief ignores important data.

For example, according to the American Psychiatric Association (2013), women suffer from major depressive disorder up to three times as often as men. The APA also reports that women suffer social anxiety, panic disorder, agoraphobia (fear of public places), and generalized anxiety disorder twice as often as men.

That sounds grim for women, but there's more to the story. While men are infrequently diagnosed with depression or anxiety, they are more than twice as likely as women to abuse alcohol or other substances. As it happens, substance abuse frequently accompanies psychiatric diagnoses like depression and anxiety (Compton et al. 2007).

Nearly twenty years ago, researchers noticed that rates of depression among women, and alcohol abuse among men, were nearly mirror-opposites (Hanna and Grant 1997). It appears that while women take their emotional difficulties to their physician or therapist, men take their problems to the pub. The astute observer can reasonably conclude that men are less frequently diagnosed with depression in part because we're more likely than women to dull our pain with substances.

Men also commit suicide far more than women, dying by their own hand twice as often as women in Western Europe, and four times as often in the United States. Men reach the threshold of suicide more quickly than women, and they complete the act more efficiently (Schrijvers, Bollen, and Sabbe 2012).

Sorry, that's pretty heavy stuff, but it's important to have a basic understanding of the mental health issues men face because those issues affect our ability to function as romantic partners. Let's turn our attention to the meaning of all this in the search for a relationship-ready man.

Despite the common notion that men are less emotional, we have the same emotional equipment as women, and the same vulnerabilities. We're simply taught to handle emotions differently. We are trained to hide emotional struggles and to avoid seeking help. As a result, we're likelier to end up as suicide or substance-abuse statistics than participants in depression and anxiety studies.

Manly stoicism and a fix-it-yourself attitude are great assets, right up to the moment when they make matters worse. That's when a man needs to be willing and able to seek assistance. Ironically, an inflexible, "manly," fix-it-yourself attitude can make him a less-than-ideal partner during life's biggest hurdles.

While we're on the rather morbid topic of male suicide, the men likeliest to attempt the act are those who feel helpless against their problems, or who are so depressed they can't muster the gumption to tackle them (Tsirigotis, Gruszczyński, and Tsirigotis-Maniecka 2014). Ironically, the man who is willing to admit to his suffering ends up being the greater survivor.

Emotional struggles don't necessarily damage a man's emotional fitness, but the unwillingness to struggle does. The relationship-ready man isn't the man who never experiences emotional turbulence. He's the man who is willing to face it head-on.

Isabel and Jack: Married to a Grump

It was a random Thursday evening when Isabel threatened to divorce her husband, Jack. She simply wasn't willing to tolerate any more of his angry outbursts.

His latest eruption came after he learned that Isabel and their ten-year-old son had exchanged a piece of hockey equipment Jack had purchased for the boy. He was livid for reasons Isabel couldn't discern and Jack couldn't explain. He went on a nonsensical tirade about money and respect, raising his voice and threatening to forbid their son from playing hockey.

He later tried to make amends, but these unpredictable outbursts, usually followed by an irritated apology, had become a pattern of increasing intensity in recent years. And when he wasn't angry, he was often sullen and crabby. This outburst was the last straw for Isabel. Jack's mounting irritability was making their son anxious, and it was making Isabel miserable. She threatened to divorce him if he didn't overcome his moodiness and anger.

It hadn't always been this way. Jack was essentially a happy person when they married thirteen years earlier, though he had always been prone to judging himself and his accomplishments harshly. He had never been easygoing or carefree, but he had been kind and quick to make Isabel smile.

Jack became more serious and self-critical after their son was born. Privately, he worried about his ability to provide. A few years into the marriage, Jack was denied a promotion, and his career began to stagnate. His mood at home turned from sullen to sour. Little, unpredictable events would make him pouty or angry. Whether it was an unpleasant experience at a restaurant, or a mildly critical word from Isabel, Jack seemed to have lost his ability to tolerate even mild disappointment.

Isabel urged him to begin therapy, or at least discuss his irritability with his physician. Jack always declined, saying they didn't have the money for therapy, and the doctor would only prescribe antidepressants, which he didn't want to take. In reality, he was making excuses because he didn't want to acknowledge or fix his mounting anger. He already judged himself to be a failure (it was one of his core beliefs), and he feared what he might discover about himself if he faced up to his volatility.

Now he had no choice. After several years of escalating unpleasantness Isabel had drawn a line. She told him their son was suffering because of Jack's behavior, and she had been walking on eggshells for years. She simply wasn't willing to go on living this way.

Jack finally understood the cost his behavior was exacting on others. He found a psychologist who quickly identified fear of the future and disappointment in himself as the source of his irritability. The hostility he directed at others was a reflection of core beliefs about himself.

Jack's disappointment seemed to be rooted in his relationship with his father, a high-powered physician who was constantly critical of Jack. At an early age Jack began to view himself with the same hypercritical eye. Even minor disappointments became insufferable when he viewed himself through his father's lens of impossibly high standards.

With hard work, Jack and the psychologist devised ways to become more tolerant of himself and his performance, and to insulate Isabel and their son from his pain.

His story has a happy ending. The marriage survived, and he became a more loving father and husband. It could have happened sooner, before he wasted years making his loved ones anxious and unhappy, but it sometimes takes a while for men to resolve their ambivalence about emotions. In the end, Jack and Isabel's marriage was stronger than ever.

Male Mental Health

Men are trained to keep "soft" feelings like sadness and fear under wraps. Most of us learn to cover them with "strong" feelings like anger, happiness, or indifference. Stoicism is useful, as we'll discuss in part 3, but useful stoicism and harmful avoidance can be two sides of the same coin. The man who won't confront his demons forces those around him to suffer for his lack of effort.

Jack's self-denigrating thoughts were the smaller portion of his battle. The greater challenge was simply to face his emotional side. His father had taught him to hide any appearance of weakness. Jack struggled to overcome that training, and he felt that seeking help from an outsider was a sign of weakness.

Some men don't even realize when emotional challenges are the source of their problems because the male stigma against displaying vulnerability is so strong. As Jack demonstrated, this attempt at strength can weaken men when it prevents them from seeking assistance.

In this chapter, we'll focus on the most common emotional problems among men, and the threats they pose to his relationship fitness:

- depression and anxiety
- substance abuse
- unresolved emotional injuries

We've already discussed the disparity in depression and anxiety diagnoses between men and women. Many people, including a fair number of clinicians, don't realize that men typically express depression and anxiety quite differently than women.

Men in most cultures are expected to learn strategies for distancing themselves from unpleasant emotion—skills like focusing attention away from the source of discomfort, or replacing unpleasant thoughts with more palatable ones (Davis et al. 2012). Actually, these are wonderful skills. Everyone should learn them. But they don't immunize men against depression. They can lead to real problems when men rely on them exclusively.

Unfortunately, mental health problems in men rarely have a straightforward appearance. Depression is the perfect example.

Researchers tend to focus on the cognitive and emotional symptoms of depression, such as low mood, guilt, sense of worthlessness, poor concentration, and other symptoms that are only experienced inside the skin. Depressed women typically don't hesitate to report these symptoms, hence the APA and other health organizations report the gender-based disparity we've discussed.

But when researchers measure the *effects* of depression—symptoms that can be measured outside the skin—the ratio of depressed men and women equalizes (Maier et al. 1999). These effects include problems like loss of interest in previously enjoyed activities, low sex drive, irritability, withdrawal, substance abuse, sleep problems, and so on. It's reasonable to think of these social impairments as the male expression of depression and anxiety.

Because researchers and clinicians focus on the emotional experience of depression more than the daily effects, a whole lot of depressed and anxious men like Jack don't receive proper diagnosis or treatment. Like Jack, those guys often end up taking it out on themselves and their loved ones.

In general, women are simply more willing to seek help, and they're more likely to receive a proper diagnosis from healthcare professionals. It begins in childhood, when roughly 18 percent of adolescent girls fit the APA's diagnostic criteria for a mood disorder, while only about 10 percent of boys fit the same criteria.

Is it because boys have 8 percent fewer emotional struggles? Unlikely. Rather than being diagnosed with emotional difficulties, about 23 percent of boys are diagnosed with a behavioral disorder, compared to 15 percent of girls (Merikangas et al. 2010). In other words, girls are diagnosed as *sad* and boys are labeled as *bad* in a statistically dubious, eight-point diagnostic swing. Why?

The answer probably lies in the way we measure depression among kids. One of the most common depression inventories for children has been shown to seriously underestimate depression in adolescent boys (van Beek et al. 2012).

Van Beek found that girls worry about the future, internalize blame, are self-deprecating, and report feeling sad. Boys, on the other hand, are more likely to have thoughts like *I wish I were dead*, or to externalize their sadness into behavioral problems and defiant behavior.

Perhaps it's no surprise that 13 percent of boys are diagnosed with ADHD, whereas 4.2 percent of girls receive the diagnosis. Some of those boys with ADHD diagnoses are simply showing the signs of their emotional discomfort.

This diagnostic difference both reflects and influences the way boys exhibit emotional difficulties. When a girl's behavior says *I'm struggling*, the culture and the medical community are likely to respond by saying, "Let's make you feel better." But boys are more likely to hear, "You are acting like a jerk, and you better straighten up."

Sometimes that's the correct message. But sometimes it leads to the type of emotional avoidance Jack showed. That's why these diagnostic numbers have a practical implication for relationships.

Depressed men don't necessarily look depressed. Beginning in childhood we teach men to mislabel and mistreat their emotions.

While men and women are in reality depressed in similar numbers, depressed behavior in men are likelier to include anger, substance abuse, and risk taking rather than "traditional" depressed behaviors such as withdrawing from friends and fun (Martin, Neighbors, and Griffith 2013). Informed mental health workers recognize these "masked" symptoms as a way for men to hide emotional pain.

Depressed men are 2.5 times likelier than women to respond to depression with alcohol, 2.75 times more likely to respond with cannabis, and 3 times as likely to turn to heroin or develop a gambling disorder (APA 2013). And according to the US government, as mentioned earlier, men are four times as likely as women to commit suicide (Centers for Disease Control and Prevention 2012). Those unfortunate men rarely receive mental health treatment prior to killing themselves, and their suicides frequently follow the sudden loss of a relationship, job, or home (Coleman, Kaplan, and Casey 2011).

By now, we know what depression *doesn't* look like in men, so what *does* it look like? It usually looks a lot like Jack's behavior. Let's look at an example presented by a pair of psychology researchers.

Rabinowitz and Cochran (2008) described the case of a depressed, middle-aged man who reported none of the standard symptoms like low mood, excessive sleep, or feelings of worthlessness. Though he was tormented by failed relationships, a stressful upbringing, and doubts about himself, he hid his suffering impeccably.

Publicly, he was gregarious and even inspirational to others. Privately, he was so tormented that he eventually attempted suicide, much to the surprise of friends, family, and health-care professionals. He appeared the picture of strength to all of them. He had been so well-trained to hide his suffering that he did not acknowledge his depression for what it was, and he was unwilling to accept real help.

Rabinowitz and Cochran proposed several masculine-specific features for depression:

- increased anger and interpersonal conflict
- feeling that they are failing to be "strong, self-reliant, in control, and emotionally restrained"
- work-related problems and conflicts
- hypersensitivity to perceived threats to self-esteem and self-respect
- antisocial and narcissistic traits
- alcohol and drug abuse

That list is quite different from the way in which most people think of depression. In my clinical experience, if there's one word that sums up most cases of male depression, it is *irritability*.

That may be partly because irritability, as a core symptom, interferes with work and other obligations less than sadness does (Kovess-Masfety et al. 2013). If it doesn't impair performance, then it doesn't look like depression. So goes male logic. And if it doesn't look like depression, it won't be treated like depression. So goes reality.

To further cloud the diagnostic picture, grumpy men like Jack elicit little sympathy, and they're therefore less likely to receive the proper help. It's the adult version of the depressed boy whose real problems are ignored because he is labeled with a conduct disorder.

We've focused on depression, but the same male behaviors would apply in many cases if we substituted the word "anxiety" for "depression. "

In some cases, such as with phobias and posttraumatic stress disorder, men and women suffer anxiety in equal measure and in similar ways. But most anxiety disorders are not easily categorized. They're often inseparably intertwined with depression. The International Classification of Diseases even includes a diagnosis for mixed anxiety and depression. The acknowledgment that they can be two sides of the same coin is especially pertinent to men.

Nobody chooses to become depressed or anxious, though we choose how we respond to the challenge. Unfortunately, a man who is unwilling to face his emotional challenges is simply less fit for relationships than he otherwise would be. A lot of men, like Jack, are ambivalent about seeking help. Hopefully, they resolve their ambivalence quickly, because the man who won't face his own problems leaves them for you to fix. You probably have better things to do.

Jack was a complex case because he took so danged long to settle his ambivalence, and people suffered while they were waiting. In part three, I'll offer plenty of ways to assess a man's capacity for handling emotional challenges in the hopes you can avoid being in Isabel's position. For now, let's look at the second relationship-shattering mental health problem.

SUBSTANCE ABUSE

There is probably no single, greater delineator between healthy and unhealthy relationships than the presence of drug and alcohol abuse. These are relationship killers. While men and women are similarly prone to substance abuse, men are more prone to using drugs and alcohol specifically to escape emotional pain. Alcohol is particularly menacing for men.

Across cultures, men consume more alcohol than women and wreak more havoc in the process (Holmila and Raitasalo 2005). Men often associate heavy drinking with manliness, and we frequently encourage each other to minimize the problems caused by drinking. You can hear it in the jokes men tell: "What's a man's definition of a balanced diet? A beer in each hand!" and "Chemically speaking, alcohol is a solution!" We men are masters at turning mountains into molehills.

Men also begin drinking at a younger age, they become dependent on alcohol more quickly than women, and they are less likely than women to seek treatment (Keyes et al. 2010). Men in midlife are likelier to turn to alcohol when they have a history of psychiatric problems such as major depression, generalized anxiety disorder, or posttraumatic stress disorder (Blonigen et al. 2013). We obviously compound our underlying problems when we use alcohol as a means of containing them.

Alcohol is insidious. Its presence can go virtually undetected until a man's life begins to fall apart. The problems usually start small. Maybe he gets in trouble at work, or his wife grumbles because he's neglecting his children. With time, the problems grow. He gets a DUI, or loses his job. He looks bad. He smells bad. He lies to cover his behavior, and eventually his life is immersed in shame. Alcohol seems to compel people to paint a rosy picture right up to the moment they can no longer disguise their misery and defeat.

This is relevant to relationships because alcoholism can fester for years or decades before people label and confront it. It can destroy financial security and happiness. It can hurt children, who grow up around the chaos and unpredictability of a substance-abusing parent. And alcohol-addled disinhibition can lead to serious legal problems, medical complications, and even domestic violence.

It's easy to pretend everything is OK when one is hitched to an alcoholic, but eventually the pain and destructiveness of this drug sets in. As tempting as it might be to gloss over it, an alcoholic simply cannot be fully present in a relationship.

I think we can skip the discussion of harder drugs like heroin and methamphetamine because they quickly and utterly destroy lives and devastate intimate relationships. There is no room for real human connection while a person is addicted to those substances.

But there is another drug that looks benign but can cause tremendous damage in relationships: marijuana. While pot is far less devastating than its ugly cousins, the person who relies on it cannot meet his (or her) potential as a partner.

At the time of this writing, pot is experiencing its greatest surge in popularity since Cheech and Chong, and states are beginning to legalize it. Even if you're not interested in marijuana, the man you're interested in may be.

I've seen too many people accept their partner's protestation that their daily pot use has no deleterious effect. Don't buy it if a man tries that line on you. Research findings tell a different story. Marijuana can decimate the best parts of a man and a relationship.

Regular pot use has a neutering effect on men. It lowers IQ (Meier et al. 2012), it damages memory (Solowij and Battisti 2008), it impairs decision making (Tamm et al. 2013), it devastates motivation (Treadway et al. 2012; Smirnov and Kiyatkin 2008; Bloomfield et al. 2014), and it increases anxiety (Zvolensky et al. 2008). Finally, no matter what you might have heard, pot is addictive (Hirvonen et al. 2011).

I'm no moral scold, and I have nothing against pot. Like alcohol, occasional use is mostly harmless. And unlike alcohol, pot has some legitimate medical applications. But daily, recreational use is another story. A slow-witted, unmotivated pot addict is the furthest thing from a solid partner. I have seen marijuana ruin marriages, businesses, and friendships.

A man with a drug or alcohol problem isn't necessarily unskilled at relationships. People in substance-abuse recovery can be far wiser and more insightful for having gone through the experience.

But few problems will devastate relationships like the refusal to honestly face substance-abuse problems. When one partner is in a relationship with drugs or alcohol, there is little room for other relationships. Life becomes hellish for the addict's partner, beginning with little problems like neglected housework, missed car payments, or setbacks at work. The partner of an addict or alcoholic finds him- or herself increasingly covering for shortcomings and social lapses.

For the male addict, the key to recovery is his willingness to address it in an open, committed, meaningful way. The only successful response is complete honesty, which means a willingness to tackle shame and any underlying matters like depression or anxiety. Personally, I would accept nothing less in an addicted partner than full participation in structured and regular treatment, possibly with lifelong, ongoing support.

Don't be fooled by a man who is clearly denying the heavy toll that a substance is taking on his life. Substances can turn otherwise wonderful people into top-tier liars and manipulators against their will. It's easy to be lulled into false security, even to become an unwilling participant in his avoidance.

In part 3, we'll look at ways to assess a man's relationship with substances. Words and deeds often conflict where substances are concerned, and so we will discuss ways to cut through deception. For now, here's our third relationship killer.

UNRESOLVED EMOTIONAL INJURIES

One of the primary jobs of the human mind is to learn what's dangerous in the world and prevent us from reexperiencing old injuries. It is a miraculous safety system. There would be few accidents if cars, trains, and airplanes learned from mishaps the way the human mind does.

There is also a downside to the mind's protective programming. It can actually make people *more* prone to repeating old injuries if we don't supervise it. Let's call it "the bruised-knuckle effect."

Imagine a cold day when a man is working on his car, tightening the bolt on a head gasket. (This may have happened to Yours Truly in his younger days.) The cold makes his hands slow and clumsy. The wrench slips and he raps his knuckles hard on the cold metal engine block. The pain is magnified by the icy temperature. Pained dancing and cursing ensues.

For the rest of his life, his mind will recall the incident anytime the context is similar. If it is cold, and if he is working with his hands, his mind will flash to images of the bruised-knuckle incident so many years ago. Though he might not consciously recall it, the memory will alter his behavior to avoid future bruised knuckles.

We know the mind's intent: don't repeat the injury. Problem is, the intent sometimes backfires. The memory might cause him to get skittish and anxious, paradoxically hindering his performance, which *increases* his chance of repeating the injury through awkward, hesitant behavior. Reasonable caution can grow into anxiety, and anxiety can cause clumsiness.

The solution to the mind's overcorrective nature is to put words to our experiences. Words help us balance the mind's emotion-based reactions and anxieties. The guy with the bruised knuckles might say to himself, *I need to be mindful of the torque I apply to the wrench when it's cold because the temperature affects my dexterity, sensory perception, and frustration tolerance. The temperature can also alter the way the tool interacts with the metal, so in future situations I will be more cautious.* He can easily under- or overcorrect when he fails to supervise the mind in such a direct manner.

The mind approaches emotional injuries similarly, and men are at special risk for repeating old emotional injuries thanks to the training that teaches us to *avoid* feelings rather than *supervise* their effect.

Suppose a man had a mother who punished him severely and unpredictably when she was angry. (This did not happen to Yours Truly.) His mind's natural reaction might be to avoid making *any* woman angry, *ever.*

That overcorrection would lead him to avoid necessary conversations under the erroneous assumption *all* women will behave as his mother did. Just like the man with the wrench, his inflexible avoidance of past injury would paradoxically *increase* the likelihood of conflict because he would deprive himself and his partner of the opportunity to solve problems while they were still manageable.

Rather than sinking into utter, unproductive avoidance, he would be wiser to put words to his experience, just as he would with a torque wrench: *I need to be aware that* this *woman does not react like my mother did, and therefore it is safe to communicate with her. That was then, and this is now. By avoiding conversation, I will only succeed in creating more conflict.*

Insight requires work, and acting upon it requires sustained effort. Unfortunately, we men are taught to stuff our pain, whether it's about bruised knuckles or bruised emotions. Pain tolerance is a wonderful skill—right up to the moment it predisposes us to repeat the past.

Introspection can also be taken to extremes when a person learns only to dwell on the past, failing to develop the skills to move forward in the present. People who function well in relationships tend to possess both insight and the ability to turn away from unpleasantness when doing so is the most useful course of action.

Ironically, the person who cannot stop dwelling in the past, and the person who cannot face the past, end up in a similar predicament. In each case, *now* is governed by *then*. Relationship-ready men understand their emotional history, and they don't allow it to rule the present. They have overcome the bruised-knuckle effect, and they're better partners for it.

Good Men Struggle

Stoicism is a wonderful survival mechanism and a great relationship asset. It only becomes a burden when men believe stoicism means avoiding any appearance of vulnerability or struggle. The stoic-at-all-expense mindset, which runs deep in so many male cultures, perpetuates the kinds of mental health, substance abuse, and emotional problems we've discussed in this chapter.

None of these emotional obstacles necessarily damage a man's relationship fitness. Some of the best candidates for relationships are those who are learning to manage mental or emotional challenges.

Men face a serious quandary when they admit to a struggle. They might be branded as mentally ill or emotionally weak, which can damage a man's standing with other men and with the opposite sex. Some men won't even tell their trusty physician that they're struggling, let alone their loved ones who depend on them to be strong.

The manliest act I've seen is to face those fears in the service of becoming an even better man. It shows he possesses the coping skills necessary to overcome adversity and the willingness to fight for what matters. You should expect nothing less in a happy, healthy relationship.

Now let's look at the third pillar of a good man.

CHAPTER 6
EMOTIONAL MATURITY

If emotional maturity can be summed up in one idea, it's *coping skills,* the ability to handle challenges gracefully and resourcefully. Man or woman, healthy partners possess reliable coping skills.

I'll bet you have known people who hitched themselves to emotionally immature partners. Years later, they end up with kids, and property, and other real-life concerns only to discover at the worst possible moments that their partners possess the emotional maturity of a teenager. Does this happen because our friends lack common sense and good judgment? Unlikely. Emotional maturity—or the lack of it—can be tough to detect early in the relationship when coping skills aren't really being tested.

Emotional maturity is the third pillar of a good, relationship-ready man. Without this crucial piece, even the dreamiest Prince Charming will eventually become a burden to you. Emotional encumbrances can be terribly costly. They not only prevent you from meeting your full potential, they can actually reduce your level of functioning.

Poverty, for example, is one of life's emotional millstones. A 2013 study (Mani et al.) examined poverty's draining effect on the intellect. The authors explained that "poverty-related concerns consume mental resources, leaving less for other tasks." Poverty also magnifies the effects of mistakes. There's less cushion for unexpected bills, financial errors, unplanned pregnancies, and the like.

Poverty creates an environment fraught with impediments to success, such as poor nutrition. It also taxes the mind, which reduces the quality of decisions. Poor decisions, in turn, create a more taxing environment, which leads to greater cognitive demand, and so on. This is why breaking out of poverty is such an arduous task.

An emotionally immature partner is the romantic equivalent of poverty. He taxes the intellect, and he magnifies mistakes and misfortunes. It's the wrong-man-brain-drain. Simple decisions become complex when we're forced to worry about emotional fallout; small misfortunes become large burdens when compounded by a partner's incapability and histrionics; small tasks become battles when we must carry the emotional weight of two.

All of it is mentally exhausting, and that's no mere figure of speech. Decisiveness suffers whenever we are forced to make puzzling decisions involving complex trade-offs (Vohs 2013). (Consider the unfortunate woman who must repeatedly decide whether to avoid her friends at social gatherings or face the possibility that her partner's drunken or inept behavior will embarrass her.) Our minds are easily fatigued when weighing complexities and exercising self-control, just as a cheetah is wearied by the chase and must recover before sprinting again. An emotionally immature person can lead his otherwise capable partner into a costly and exhausting vortex of drama, chaos, and pain. Just like being poverty-stricken, it's hard to climb out of that hole of romantic poverty.

Emotional maturity, on the other hand, has been shown to be a major contributor to relationship satisfaction. No surprise there.

Consider one facet of emotional maturity: emotional intelligence. That's the ability to perceive and understand emotions in others, along with the ability to understand and manage emotions in oneself.

People are happier in relationships when they have a high emotional intelligence and, just as significantly, when their partners are emotionally intelligent (Schröder-Abé and Schütz 2011). Emotional intelligence predicts relationship satisfaction, closeness, and commitment. High emotional intelligence allows people to see beyond their own momentary urgencies and understand the perspective of their partner during conflict. Who wouldn't want a partner who can handle challenges with grace and empathy?

Even relationship conflicts with an emotionally mature person tend to have productive resolutions, leaving both partners wiser and happier. Just as emotional immaturity can stunt your potential, a mature partner can increase it.

Partnering with an emotionally immature man can create terrible struggles years down the road when life gets complicated. It's mighty advantageous to recognize these men early in the relationship, before their emotional reserves are truly put to the test. Dating is like a job interview, where even the worst employee can make a great first impression. The real test comes later.

Consider Jimmy, the last of our cautionary tales among the three pillars. He lacks emotional maturity, and it shows in even his most basic relationships.

Sarah and Jimmy: Not What He Seems

Sarah met Jimmy while working at a large home improvement store. She was an inventory manager, and he was a team leader on the sales floor. He was handsome and charismatic, and he had been promoted quickly to team leader. He seemed like Mr. Reliable.

Jimmy had big goals and big ideas that extended far beyond the home improvement store. He often talked about the relationships he claimed to have with influential people and the special paths to wealth and influence that were open to him. He felt he deserved success, and he boasted that he would not rest until he had met his goals. Sarah liked his confidence.

Despite his rapid promotion, Jimmy's job at the store was short-lived. He was fired after a run-in with a manager. Some of his coworkers were surprised. Others said they saw it coming because Jimmy was quick to anger when he was challenged or corrected.

He had other less-than-admirable habits, like his tendency to complain about superiors behind their backs. That was just one of several destructive patterns that were not apparent during his first few months of employment. When Sarah and he spoke about his firing, he convinced her (and himself) that the company treated him unfairly.

After his firing, he would sometimes complain to Sarah for hours about his "incompetent" managers. The company simply hadn't seen the value in him or his ideas, he said as he ruminated on the thought he had been mistreated. He eventually decided he was better off for being fired. He would find an employer who appreciated all he had to offer.

Sarah began to notice something missing in Jimmy's view of the world. His explanations were one-sided and self-serving. He seemed unwilling to examine his role in conflict. Nevertheless, she once again overlooked his lack of introspection, focusing instead on his wounded emotions. She reminded herself he was an intelligent man with big goals. She convinced herself such people are commonly misunderstood.

Jimmy found another job, and over the course of the next year he followed the same trajectory: rapid promotions followed by a quick decline as he became disenchanted with his employer. He spent an inordinate amount of time complaining to Sarah about the shortcomings of his managers and coworkers. Tensions mounted with his employer, as they had at the home improvement store, and Jimmy eventually resigned.

Sarah had been dating him for more than a year, and the pattern was becoming impossible to ignore. It wasn't just jobs; his friendships seemed to follow a similar course.

He would meet new people at his job or in his softball league and form quick alliances. He idealized his new friends at first, but inevitably they would fall from grace in his estimation. He would complain bitterly to Sarah about their shortcomings and the disrespect they showed toward him.

One memorable day he obsessed for hours about a friend who neglected to invite him to a football party. He felt the friend was socially indebted to him, and he couldn't understand why he was being so mistreated.

Increasingly, Sarah served as his sounding board while he complained about the shortcomings of employers, friends, and even family. She had grown to endure it patiently, asking little in return.

Then came the time when she needed him to be emotionally supportive. She was unexpectedly laid off from the home improvement store. She found herself in a financial mess, with a mortgage and a student loan to cover each month. She didn't want to turn to her family because they were struggling with their own adversity. That left Jimmy. She didn't want to be financially rescued. She simply needed him to listen and to be strong and steady, as she had done for him so many times.

An emotional tug-of-war developed as he routinely overruled her sadness with his own complaints. If she was lamenting an unsuccessful job interview, he would one-up her by complaining about his boss. If she expressed sadness about applying for unemployment, he trumped her sadness with anger about anything from politics to his parents. If she became anxious about how to pay her mortgage, he would insensitively burden her with his own lesser financial concerns.

In other words, the more she needed him, the needier and more demanding he became. It was as if he believed emotional support was a scarce commodity, and he saw her as a competitor for limited resources.

Sarah realized she was fighting on two fronts. Not only was she dealing with her own frustrating job search, but she also carried the emotional burden Jimmy was becoming. His behavior was stressful and depressing. His emotional immaturity only increased the challenge of finding a new job. Far from being helpful, her interactions with Jimmy left her feeling physically and emotionally drained.

Finally, she realized she needed to end the relationship, as had so many employers and friends before her. Jimmy was hurt and angry after the breakup, openly complaining to anyone who would listen and sending vitriolic text messages to Sarah accusing her of being self-centered and incapable of real love. The irony of the accusation was not lost on her.

Still needing to find work and stability, Sarah felt more alone and vulnerable than ever. But she also felt optimistic about her future. She had shed Jimmy's emotional dead weight early in the relationship while it was still relatively easy to escape.

The Emotionally Mature Man

Jimmy attracted people with a great first impression, but then lost his composure when challenges appeared. I hope Jimmy eventually developed the emotional skills he needed. I'm also thankful Sarah didn't build a life and family with him. As charming and smart as he may have been, he lacked the resources to remain connected to people when their needs took the spotlight.

Such a shortcoming is one of the telltale signs of emotional immaturity. But what does an emotionally *mature* man look like?

Here is the first and most important fact about emotionally mature men: we don't necessarily behave like emotionally mature women. Why would we? We have different emotional predispositions and we receive different training.

This is a common source of friction in couples. Women often expect men to act like women. *Why can't he be more sensitive?* And men often wish women would think more like men. *Why can't she just forget it and move on?* The wise couple accepts and appreciates their differences.

Despite the differences, men and women share several traits of emotional maturity. Here's a short list of some bare-minimum emotional skills women *and* men should seek in order to avoid being trapped with someone like Jimmy. Emotionally mature mates should be able to do several things:

- describe emotional experiences in themselves
- intuit the emotional states of others
- tolerate discomfort without turning to destructive escapes like drugs and alcohol
- tolerate emotional distress without becoming hostile
- get their needs met without being manipulative
- calm themselves when they are overcome with emotions like anger or sadness
- take care of themselves physically and emotionally
- control impulses and solve problems constructively, especially when emotions are high
- make wise decisions rather than impetuous choices driven by emotion
- adapt to challenging situations rather than demanding the situation adapt to them
- possess a clear sense of values that serves to temper emotions and guide decision making
- accept the occasional unfairness of life and be able to function in an unfair world

In addition to these basic skills, there are some special considerations for men since we are usually trained to minimize and avoid "soft" emotions like sadness. The emotionally mature man possesses these characteristics:

- an ability to identify and help others understand his emotional experiences, even if he's hesitant to discuss them further
- the resilience to withstand emotional discomfort without retreating or abandoning others
- the self-efficacy to admit imperfections and errors

There's one more trait to look for: resourcefulness. You might not think of it as an emotional skill, but it is a hallmark of male emotional maturity. It's so important it gets its own section.

WHY RESOURCEFULNESS MATTERS IN A MAN

Resourcefulness is the ability to solve problems with efficiency and ingenuity. The resourceful man is capable. He's enterprising. He's curious and inventive.

We've already discussed how crucial it is for men to possess a sense of effectiveness in their professional and social lives. Resourcefulness is like rocket fuel for a man's sense of effectiveness. The more skillful he is at handling problems, the more effective he is in the world.

This extends to relationships, too. *Real* men aren't merely good at fixing cars and houses. They aren't simply Johnny-on-the-spot when a friend needs help. They also possess emotional resourcefulness. They're quicker at resolving quarrels, and they're able to avoid common relationship traps.

One of the most common relationship pitfalls is what some psychologists call it the "retreat-pursuit pattern." It works like this. Imagine some miscellaneous bit of tension arises in a relationship. One partner (often the man) wants to escape the discomfort of talking about it. We'll call this person the retreater. The other partner (often the woman) wants to discuss it at length. We'll call that person the pursuer.

These two people are at odds from the start. The retreater feels anxiety at the thought of discussing the problem; the pursuer feels anxiety at the thought of *not* discussing it. You can see the quandary. The more the pursuer pursues, the more anxious the retreater becomes. The more the retreater retreats, the more anxious the pursuer is.

There are several reasons why the woman in a couple is usually the pursuer and the man is usually the retreater. For one, men and women have slightly different autonomic (fight-or-flight) responses. Because of its role in mobilizing us for the fight, the autonomic nervous system (ANS) has big implications in lovers' quarrels.

During an argument, the ANS can trigger physical reactions designed to help us respond to more serious threats. It gives us elevated heart rate, shunting of blood to the muscles, increased respiration, and so on. This adrenal response is wonderfully useful when we need to evade or defeat a physical threat, but it is clearly unhelpful during a discussion with a romantic partner. Nevertheless, our bodies sometimes prepare us for fight or flight even when we have no desire to battle or flee from our loved ones.

This fight-or-flight response involves two-way communication between the brain and the body. While the brain is the ultimate arbiter, it also monitors the body for these signs of stress, like a supervisor checking in with the front-line crew. When it notices the body is experiencing signs of stress (shaking, sweating, and so forth), the brain is a little less willing to give up the fight. It is as if the brain is saying, *My body is still upset, so there must be something to be upset about.*

When a man's ANS is recovering from fight-or-flight mode, his body is sending a subtle signal to his brain that the threat has subsided. His brain interprets this to mean it's time to kiss and make up.

But women recover from autonomic arousal more slowly than men (Sapolsky 2005). While he's calming down, she might still be in fight-or-flight mode, her body telling her brain that the fight is still on. In other words, when he's in biological retreat mode, she may still be in biological fight mode. The differences between men and women are usually wonderfully complementary, but this bit of asynchrony is unfortunate when we're in the midst of conflict.

Here's a second contributor to the retreat-pursuit pattern. While men are trained to avoid distressing internal experiences like fear or sadness, women are more likely to embrace and explore those feelings.

In 2012, a group of researchers (Davis et al.) showed men and women disturbing photos designed to elicit negative emotions such as revulsion or sadness. Then the researchers measured each gender's emotional responses and noticed that women reported higher levels of emotion than the men.

That doesn't mean the men were less able to experience emotion than the women. It simply means they handled their emotions in a way that created a lower response to the distressing images.

The researchers discovered that the men reported less emotion in part because they quickly moved away from their feelings by engaging in emotional distancing strategies. For example, some men avoided dwelling on the pictures and steered their minds toward other thoughts. Some men shifted their attention away from the unpleasant focal point to more benign details of the picture. Many of them even exercised control over their facial expression, which helps contain emotional reactions.

The female participants, on the other hand, faced their emotions rather than retreating from them. Women were more likely to explore the nature and the source of their emotions. The men might say the women dwelled unnecessarily, while the women might say the men were emotionally avoidant.

Which approach is better? Neither, in my opinion. They both have their uses. But this is another male-female difference that can contribute to the retreat-pursuit pattern. He may be actively trying to avoid an unpleasant idea or argument, while she is trying to face it head-on. Each approach can frustrate the heck out of the other person.

A third contributor to the retreat-pursuit pattern is the differences in the way men and women experience anxiety.

Across cultures, women appear to be more prone to anxiety than men. (Our previous discussion of diagnostic rates notwithstanding; this difference appears to be genuine rather than an artifact of poor diagnosis.) McLean and Anderson (2009) compiled several reasons for the disparity, including some that are relevant to the retreat-pursuit pattern.

Among them, women are more likely to overestimate the probability of awful outcomes, ruminate over painful emotions, and vicariously experience other people's unpleasant feelings. This may contribute to a woman's perception that men are oblivious to friction, as well as a man's perception that women ruminate on problems they should ignore.

Add different emotional training to those three contributors, and it is no wonder men and women are so prone to the pursuit-retreat pattern. Nature and society have stacked the deck, which brings us back to the importance of resourcefulness.

In the epic poem *The Odyssey*, the hero Odysseus faced deadly traps on his return home from the Trojan War. There was the Cyclops who would crush him, the Sirens who would drive him insane, the Charybdis who would swallow his ships, and other dangers that had claimed the lives of those who tried to pass. But they did not claim resourceful Odysseus because he outsmarted every adversary and evaded every trap.

Resourceful Odysseus was never really in danger because he knew he had options, and he's the kind of guy who wouldn't have fallen into the retreat-pursuit pattern. A good man is aware of his options in the realm of emotion and intimacy.

Even if he has a history of limited emotional training, a good man wants to expand his skills. He's not going to let biology, training, or culture impede his happiness. When problems like the retreat-pursuit pattern show up, the resourceful man wants to identify them, face them, and fix them as a team.

IT'S ALL ABOUT OPTIONS

Some women view emotional flexibility as a luxury in a man, but it is more of a necessity. Men and women who understand their emotional options are simply better at resolving conflict. The power of emotional flexibility begins in childhood.

For example, one school-based program significantly reduced aggression in violent adolescents (159 boys and 8 girls) by helping them recognize options other than violence for handling aggressive thoughts and feelings (Ronen and Rosenbaum 2010).

How did the researchers do it? They simply helped kids to put words to their emotions, teaching them to understand the link between feelings and behavior. This basic insight is a developmental milestone for adolescents, but not every adolescent reaches it.

With that insight in place, the researchers then taught more advanced self-control skills such as delaying temptation, using self-talk, and strategizing about goals. In other words, they showed the kids there were many options concerning their emotions. As a result, the children became more emotionally resourceful.

Not only did violence decrease. Their study habits improved, and they reported better relationships with friends. For those children, emotional resourcefulness was life-changing.

For many men, nuanced emotional dealings are foreign territory. It takes a courageous man to enter those waters, especially when he has been specifically trained against it. Courage is one of the many traits emotionally mature men possess. And where do men learn traits such as courage? Usually, from other men.

THIRTEEN RELATIONSHIP SKILLS MEN TEACH BOYS

Remember Jimmy from the beginning of this chapter? His relationships started well, but he had trouble maintaining them, and that made him poor boyfriend material. Emotionally, he was a boy in a man's body.

Have you ever watched little boys? They are overflowing with curiosity, joy, and enthusiasm. They are also greedy, self-centered, and pushy. They need to be sculpted into men. It is certainly possible for women to teach boys how to be men, but no one does a better job of it than a good man. Even when boys are cursed with fathers who mistreat or abandon them, they can make up for lost time by adopting mentors and role models.

Men help boys develop emotional maturity by teaching specific skills, sometimes in unseen ways. Believe it or not, the coaches, fathers, brothers, and uncles who inspire, cajole, tease, command, and discipline a boy are turning him into better relationship material. In my years of working with couples, I have noticed several emotional traits men teach and reinforce in each other. These manly skills make us better romantic partners.

> **Respect.** Two building blocks of respect are the ability to admire others and the willingness to defer to those who possess greater skill. These are two of the most basic skills boys learn from male role models, and they come in quite handy in romantic relationships after the boy has become a man. The ability to admire allows a man to cherish the finer points of his partner. The willingness to defer allows him to recognize the superior abilities of others and seek advice, or follow her lead, in times of need. These two components of respect are part of Manhood 101.

> **Impulse control.** Little boys are driven by impulse. That impulsiveness works great when we're young and soaking up knowledge about the world, but it must be reined in before it becomes dangerous. In relationships, impulse control prevents a man from being reckless, it allows him to plan ahead, and it keeps him from saying or doing things he'll regret.

Persistence. This is another trait from Manhood 101. We learn it from mentors and competitors alike. We teach each other not to walk away from challenges before the job is done. In relationships, this quality gives a man the wherewithal to stick with his partner through the tough times.

Humility. Many's the time a man has put a boy in his place. While it may look harsh, criticism is one of the kindest gifts a mentor or father figure can offer to a boy. Young men are prone to feelings of invincibility. Instilling a sense of humility helps boys understand their limits without getting hurt. In relationships, humility allows men to seek guidance rather than charging forward and making things worse.

Competitiveness. When I was researching *The Women's Guide to How Men Think*, one consistent theme from women was their curiosity about the male ability to shake hands and be friendly after a serious clash. Men teach each other that competition doesn't mean war. In relationships, this gives men the ability to forgive and forget.

Cooperation. As we've already discussed, men are highly cooperative with one another, more than women in some contexts. Men learn cooperation largely through competition, which is one of the reasons boys must be allowed to compete with each other. The value of a cooperative, team mentality in romantic relationships probably goes without saying.

Loyalty. Whether it is the team a man plays for, the country he fights for, or the family he lives for, principled men teach young men how to be loyal to others. The loyal man knows that disagreements don't need to end relationships.

Discipline. Every young man should master one essential fact of life before venturing into the grown-up world: sometimes it doesn't matter whether you *feel* like meeting a requirement. Get your body moving, and your heart will follow—or it won't. Either way, get the job done. Relationships are better when men understand how to overcome inertia and solve problems before they grow.

Values. Good men teach young men how to think about values, and how to make the right choice even when doing so is uncomfortable. In relationships, this gives a man the ability to be an unwavering ally for his partner.

Impeccability. Good men teach young men to keep their commitments and their word. Men who lack this skill create headaches and heartaches for people who depend on them. Impeccability benefits relationships because it's simply easier and more pleasant to have a solid, dependable partner who keeps his commitments.

Stoicism. Boys are reckless little critters. When they inevitably get hurt, men are more prone than women to say "walk it off" or "rub some dirt on it." There's a crucial message about character in those hard-edged messages. Discomfort shouldn't rule how we respond to the world, and distancing oneself from emotional pain is an indispensable skill. Yes, fortitude and bravery can go too far, but so can meekness and emotionality. Men are better romantic partners when they're able to face challenges with strength.

Perspective taking. Following close on the heels of stoicism is the ability to see the world from another's point of view. Good men teach young men that they are most useful when they understand the needs and motivations of others. Or to put it in manlier terms, sometimes you're right; sometimes you're acting like a jackass. An emotionally mature man knows the difference.

Flexibility. The day a young man recognizes he can be spectacularly wrong is one of the most productive days in his life. That's the day he realizes he can take correction, change course, and emerge stronger for it. Happy romantic relationships don't exist without this skill.

Good men possess these qualities in different measure, and every good man will struggle in some areas. Maybe he's too cooperative, or too competitive, or he's still learning flexibility. That's OK, because there's one more trait good men teach boys: the willingness to embrace the struggle. A good man is aware of his strengths and weaknesses, and he knows he is a work in progress. Beware the Jimmys of the world who believe they are a masterpiece of emotional perfection.

Seeing What Isn't There

Emotional maturity is one of the most crucial factors to scrutinize when you're choosing someone with whom to spend a lifetime. You'll need him in your corner someday, and you won't want to be weighed down by someone with Jimmy's immaturity. You'll want resourcefulness, flexibility, and impeccability.

Just as importantly, the time will inevitably arrive when you need to negotiate a significant conflict with him. Qualities like respect and loyalty will help you both find the win-win solution.

And, God forbid, should life ever saddle you with serious misfortune, a dependable man will be persistent and stoic in the best sense of the word. You won't have to carry his share of the load or face the burden alone. He will also possess the humility to accept your help when he needs it.

People on the dating scene who overlook these basic emotional skills do so to their own detriment. Still, some overlook them. Maybe they do so because coping skills and emotional maturity aren't flashy or obvious. They are simply useful, like having a reliable jack in the trunk of your car. Necessary, but hardly thrilling—until the day you need it.

Assessing a man's emotional maturity is sometimes an exercise in seeing what is *not* there, like drama, boastfulness, neediness, treacherousness, and other qualities people tend to hide when they are trying to forge a favorable impression.

To further obscure it, good men don't boast about their emotional prowess. It's unlikely you will hear a man who's trying to win your affection say something like, "Yeah baby, you're looking at a man who knows how to accept help when he needs it." You'll need to know what to look for.

In part 3, we will look at specific ways to assess a man's maturity, focusing heavily on the coping behaviors you can observe in his daily life. We'll examine measurable ways he conducts himself as an individual, because research shows that a man who handles adversity well on his own is likelier to handle it well when he's part of a couple (Papp and Witt 2010).

Psychologists refer to joint problem solving as *dyadic coping*. Unsurprisingly, dyadic coping is a strong predictor of relationship satisfaction (Herzberg 2013). Couples are happier when they can work toward solutions rather than becoming mired in emotional distress.

Dyadic coping is pivotal to the overall functioning of the relationship, and it affects women's relationship satisfaction more than men's (Bodenmann, Pihet, and Kayser 2006). You might even say partnership is the main point of relationships.

A Brief Review

Let's take a brief inventory of what we have covered so far. Part 1 discussed bringing your best self to the relationship. That involves some work on your part:

- understanding your history with men
- knowing your relationship patterns
- possessing a solid understanding of your values

Here in part 2, we looked at the three pillars of a good, relationship-ready man:

- a sense of purpose
- good mental health
- emotional maturity

Having come this far, you might be wondering if there are any good men out there. As someone who has seen the inner workings of a great many relationships, I can tell you unequivocally, yes. Let's go now to the 12-point man inspection, where we'll weed out the misfits and make room for the good men who are searching for you.

Part III
The 12-Point
Man Inspection

Sense of purpose, good mental health, and emotional maturity. These are the three pillars of a good man. Unfortunately, it's impractical to ask a man, "How's your sense of purpose, your mental health, and your emotional maturity?"

He might blithely reply, "Great, perfect, and better than anyone I know!"

Direct questions can yield useless information, even if he believes it himself. Let us turn instead to some old truths: his character will reveal itself over time, and his actions will tell you more than his words.

Finding the ideal partner isn't merely a decision of the heart. It is a decision of the intellect, as well. While the heart knows what it wants, only your mind can size up a man's romantic skill.

CHAPTER 7
ASSESSING HIS
SENSE OF PURPOSE

As we go forward, I'm hoping you can recite the three pillars of a good, relationship-ready man by heart: sense of purpose, good mental health, and emotional maturity. (Spread the word!) In the next three chapters, we will cover twelve questions to help you measure a man's relationship potential, beginning with the first pillar.

We've seen how men's sense of purpose can profoundly affect their romantic relationships. There was Aaron, the rudderless man, whose aimlessness created a miserable, state of affairs for himself and his partner. We also met Rob, the driven political activist. He was a man of tremendous purpose, but his values were hopelessly misaligned with those of Julia, his wife.

A man's values and his sense of purpose are intertwined. They're like beer and pretzels; biscuits and gravy; Ernie and Bert.

Since it's hard for a relationship to survive conflicting values, and since values and purpose are often woven together, we'll start here:

- Inspection Item 1: Are his values compatible with yours?

This first question is unique because it is the only one in this book having to do with whether he is an ideal fit for *you*. In the remainder of this chapter, we will examine three questions directly related to his sense of purpose:

- Inspection Item 2: Is he part of something larger than himself?
- Inspection Item 3: Is he maintaining his man card?
- Inspection Item 4: Is he striving to be honorable?

A man's sense of purpose shows itself more in what he *does* than in what he *says*. That's why this section focuses on observable behavior—where he chooses to invest his time and energy, how he defines and performs his role in society, and how he treats others. These are all related to what he hopes to accomplish in life, and who he wants to be in the world.

There is also a philosophical thread that runs through this chapter: the question of character. Lust is fun, but it fades. Attraction is vital, but it is only the start. Love is essential, but it isn't always enough. As we've seen in the cautionary tales of previous sections, character matters.

The man of purpose will usually be a man of character (unless his purpose is to succeed at the expense of others). If he has purpose, character, and his values match your own, then the relationship has the first few building blocks of a solid foundation.

INSPECTION ITEM 1: ARE HIS VALUES COMPATIBLE WITH YOURS?

Back in chapter 3, we discussed some of the research on the role of values in relationships. Here's what we know about most happy and successful couples:

- They are developed as individuals, and they are clear on their individual values before building a life together.

- They find meaning in similar activities during their time together.
- They satisfy each other's preferences for excitement or calmness.
- They have shared emotional responses to their experiences.
- They have an appreciation for each other's individual goals, and they support each other in those endeavors.
- They have a similar desire for emotional closeness.
- They are confident enough in their similarities to easily tolerate their differences.

Also in chapter 3, we looked at how our hearts and minds can be drawn to mates who are exciting, attractive, and fun for a few dates, while being entirely unsuitable for long-term relationships because their values contradict our own. There's something exciting and exotic about a person who is simultaneously attractive and challenging to our values. Oh, the romance of a love so powerful that it transcends our differences!

That works best in the movies, where the credits will roll before the couple starts resenting each other for what they've sacrificed. The heart is great at picking short-term excitement, but it's up to us to find long-term meaning and happiness.

The Secret to Assessing His Values

I'm going to share with you an ancient matchmaking technique. It is as old as civilization, and it works like a charm. Are you ready? Here it is:

Take your time and get to know each other.

"Courtship" is an old-fashioned word that has fallen out of use. I think it is worthy of resurrection.

Courtship is a period of time in which a couple gets to know each other before making serious decisions about building a life together. In some cultures, courtship is ritualized and highly structured, sometimes even governed by religion. That's fine, but it's not what

I'm talking about. By courtship, I simply mean the slow and deliberate effort to learn what makes a person tick. As old fashioned as it may sound, it's even useful to delay sex until we're certain of a partner's trustworthiness and emotional stability, because nothing brings out the worst (or the best) in a person like sex.

You might be wondering how long courtship should last. My answer is ten years. If you happen to be *my* daughter, then twenty years.

I realize a decade is impractical unless you're a sea turtle who will someday celebrate your 150th birthday, so here's a more reasonable approach. Getting to know someone probably takes longer than you think—and longer than you would like. When his thoughts and behaviors no longer surprise you, you're halfway there.

"Longer than you think" is awfully imprecise, I know. Our hearts want satisfaction *now*, which is precisely why we need to get the mind involved before becoming another cautionary tale in some psychologist's relationship book. Here are some guidelines for the slow process of discovering his values and sharing your own.

Have plenty of joy-filled conversations. Mutual discovery should be a treat. If it begins to feel like a burden or an obstacle, then the relationship may have a shaky foundation.

Be honest with yourself about his behavior, his thoughts, and his opinions. We humans have an astounding ability to hear what we wish to hear, even in the face of contrary evidence. Do yourself a favor and take him at his word if he tells you he hates your mother and loves his UFO cult group. Don't assume he will change for you or anyone else. (On the other end of the spectrum are men whose deeds do not align with the sweetness of their words. We'll be discussing those warning signs in chapter 10.)

Have candid conversations about the areas in which your values diverge. *Differing* values don't necessarily harm a relationship, but *contradictory* values often do. If one person is a devout Catholic and the other is a vocal atheist, Christmas with the kiddos is going to be unpleasant for everyone. But up to a point, *differing* values can add intellectual spice and be quite healthy for a relationship. No couple agrees on everything. The central question is, do you respect each other and your individual interests?

In our earlier values discussion, we looked at this list of value categories from the world of behavioral psychology:

- work
- leisure activity
- caregiving
- family
- intimate relationships
- community involvement
- spirituality and religion
- education and personal development
- health
- social connectedness

We added two more items to the list where romantic relationships are concerned:

- finances
- physical intimacy

These last two are major sources of conflict in couples. Let's start with money. Couples tend to fight over money when it represents something different to each partner. Perhaps it represents security to one partner while the other views it as a means to be used liberally for making memories and enjoying life. It is easy for one partner to feel that her values are under attack when the other is merely acting on his own values—and vice versa.

For example, the one who sees money as being integral to security might feel that the other is making him vulnerable to danger when she wants to spend money on a vacation. The partner who values memories and enjoyment, on the other hand, might feel that the security-driven partner is being oppressive when he wants to cut spending and pad the savings account.

In a similar way, differing values about sex can leave each partner feeling as if his or her values, and even his or her very being, is under attack. A nasty cycle of rejection can develop when one partner (not always the man) esteems physical connection as a reflection of love, while the other (not always the woman) places less importance on sex. Sometimes the more sexually driven partner ends up feeling continually rejected and withdraws affection in retaliation.

Here are a few questions to guide your assessment of his values:

Does he have a sense of where he's headed in life?

Is his vision of the future compatible with yours?

Do you enjoy the activities and conversations you share with him?
Based on your time with him so far, would you enjoy spending time with him for the rest of your life?

Do you have similar preferences for excitement and/or calmness?

Are you comfortable supporting his professional and personal goals?
Is he comfortable supporting yours?

Do you have similar desires for emotional closeness? Do you desire similar amounts of time together? Similar levels of conversational depth? Similar levels of physical affection?

Are you each confident enough in your similarities to enjoy your differences?

In case you're wondering how you're supposed to gather all this information about his values, the answer is simple: courtship. It is like a long job interview, though hopefully a lot more fun.

Relationships frequently don't survive courtship, which is really the point of it. Better to end the relationship amicably after a few months than to suffer a painful divorce after several years and a few kids. Breaking up stinks, especially when you've become fond of someone. I reckon more than a few people rush into mismatched commitments in order to avoid that harsh reality.

Courtship is worth the time, and you are worth courting. Any man who is unwilling to get to know you is unworthy of your love.

Fantasies and Self-Deception

Would you like to hear about my first car? It was a 1979 Dodge Omni, olive green with an oxidized hood and far too many miles on it. At $850, it was grossly overpriced.

I knew that car was going to be bad news, but I ignored my intuition. I bought it because I was sixteen, impatient, and broke. Sure enough, it turned out to be a money pit and an albatross.

The window crank broke. The cheap clutch cable snapped. It dropped a muffler. It even threw a rod. (If you don't know much about engines, that's about as bad as it gets.) Between major breakdowns it always had some sort of mechanical ache or pain.

My car was ugly, slow, and discouraging. I would have done well to ride my bike and save up for a nicer set of wheels, but I managed to convince myself the car represented freedom. In my imagination, this $850 lemon was perfect. It was my chariot to Happyville.

Deep down, from the moment I test-drove it, I knew better. I paid a price for ignoring intuition. On the bright side, I learned a lot about repairing cars, though there are better ways to gain that knowledge. But, really, the car was more trouble than it was worth, as are some relationships.

Humans are immensely capable of self-deception. Nowhere is this more true than in romance, where we can minimize the importance of values. *Our love will conquer all!* Common enemies and obstacles are especially disorienting because they create a special kind of romantic blindness. *It's me and him against the world!* That works until you realize you really don't respect your partner-in-arms.

Self-deception is part of the human condition. So what is the cure? Once again, judiciousness is as simple as slowing down. I could have made better decisions about transportation had I been less impetuous when I was sixteen. The same is true of romance. Deliberate courtship creates the opportunity to notice when we're trying to sell ourselves a bill of goods. It makes room for our little intuitive voice that whispers, *Hey, something doesn't feel quite right.* Self-deception rarely stands the test of time.

Time also creates the opportunity to notice *his* self-deception. We men are equally prone to fooling ourselves, and not just about cars. Women need to understand this male vulnerability to protect themselves. Kindhearted, well-intentioned men can unintentionally deceive women in the process of deceiving themselves about the fitness of a relationship.

Inspection Item 2: Is He Part of Something Larger than Himself?

It is an age-old romantic struggle. One partner wants more time alone than the other. In intense cases, it can create a constant tension in which one partner feels he or she must constantly fight for attention while the other struggles to find time alone. Often, though not always, it is the man who craves more time away from the relationship.

Researchers have shown that men and women gravitate toward different social structures. Generally speaking, we men are more drawn to large, interconnected groups than women, and we operate well within them.

Most men possess a predisposition to meet challenges as a team, particularly when their team is competing with other teams (Van Vugt, De Cremer, and Janssen 2007). Men who literally sweat together are more cooperative with each other, thanks to a pheromone in male perspiration that facilitates teamwork. And contrary to popular wisdom, high testosterone levels in men also correlate with a cooperative team mentality (Huoviala and Rantala 2013).

That means for some couples, his bowling league may support the health of their relationship more than she realizes. His male-oriented team pursuits may actually make him a better partner at home. Most men function best when they can move back and forth between group activities and intimate relationships.

While not all men possess it in equal measure, most men require some sort of outside passion in order to bring their best selves to the relationship. The wise woman realizes this is one of the wonderful areas in which men and women operate differently. In my clinical experience, men are better partners when they are part of something larger than themselves. They come home voluntarily, happily, and ready to connect.

His Sense of Balance

Though he may have team-oriented urges, the relationship-ready man seeks a healthy balance between his intimate relationship and his outside pursuits. If he's spending too much time at the office, or the dojo, or the bowling alley, then he may be sending the message that he's not ready for partnership, or that there's a problem with the relationship.

How much is "too much?" Clearly, there's no formulaic answer. The answer lies in your values. It can weaken the relationship if the balance he seeks diverges sharply from your desires. This conflict of visions is a potential source of resentment on both sides should the couple fall into an ongoing struggle over the amount of time they spend together. One partner feels abandoned while the other feels nagged—and people who feel nagged often become even more resistant.

Ideally, his outside interest fosters intimacy. For all the reasons we discussed in chapter 4, a sense of purpose makes him a better man and a better partner, especially when he knows he is free to cultivate his sense of purpose without creating discord in his relationship. Smart couples discuss the purpose and balance of each of their outside pursuits.

Inspection Item 3: Is He Maintaining His Man Card?

What is a *real* man? What does a *real* man do in the world? I think there's no more universally accepted definition than the one we discussed back in chapter 4: a real man produces more than he consumes.

No doubt some people consider this to be outmoded, paternalistic, and primitive, but it remains a foundation of the male psyche and the human experience. Men who drain society's coffers, rather than adding to them, are the subject of scorn and ridicule. Society revokes their man cards.

Whether or not this is an outmoded way of thinking about men and society would make for a lively debate at the local tavern, but we're here to discuss the ideal mate. I believe the man card is a reliable measure of a man's ability to function romantically.

Really, we should all strive to be someone who produces more than we consume in a relationship—not necessarily in material, but in devotion. Imagine the comfort and security that kind of partner brings!

A well-rounded, relationship-ready man is a generous man, both materially and emotionally. He is able to be strong when you feel vulnerable, and he's able to accept your support when the world treats him poorly. In neither case is he an emotional drain. He pulls his share of the load and then some.

A man card isn't like a high school diploma. You don't earn it once, forget it, and move on. It must be maintained, in large part by keeping oneself mentally and physically healthy. Here's how you know he takes his man card seriously and brings his best self to the relationship.

He takes care of himself. Having a man card means being useful to others, and he can't be useful to others if he's mentally or emotionally ragged. A good man works to take care of his body and mind. If he has mental or emotional difficulties, he's actively addressing them. He does these to stay healthy, not because others prod him. He wants to be sturdy, capable, and ready to go when he's needed. He may not be a specimen of physical perfection—who among us is?—but a good and healthy man doesn't neglect his basic needs.

He surrounds himself with respectable men. At work and at leisure, he associates with other men of high character. They challenge him to be a better man, sometimes merely by their presence and example. The men he chooses to surround himself with are a sign of the man he is trying to be.

He is thoughtful about others. A relationship-ready man has his own emotional house in order, which allows him to be a caring and attuned presence for others. He is aware of his friends' and loved ones' struggles. He holds the door for people; he helps his friends move; he's a rock. He might even engage in charitable acts, like coaching a children's soccer team. A good man possesses the emotional wherewithal to consider people other than himself.

Basic practices like these help to keep a man happy, healthy, and able to engage in a relationship. They show he is maintaining his man card, and he won't be burdened by stagnation, shame, and the anxiety of letting it lapse. The wise woman knows a good man takes seriously the ongoing expectation of his man card. She not only allows for the self-care it requires, she encourages it.

Inspection Item 4: Is He Striving to Be Honorable?

Since I have already turned our lexicon back a century or so with the word "courtship," allow me toss out another word that has fallen out of use: *honor*. It means being worthy of respect and admiration, even when doing so is uncomfortable.

Long ago, honor needed to be assiduously defended because allowing one's reputation to slide into disrepute could literally threaten survival. Imagine living in an isolated, preindustrial society in which others wouldn't deal with a man if they feared being mistreated or manipulated by him. In the worst case, the resources and protection of the group could be closed off to him. Men had to carefully demonstrate their trustworthiness, which required them to be mindful of others' interests.

Little has changed, really. Honor isn't a matter of life and death to most of us in the modern world, which is why some men disregard their reputations, but society still accommodates those who maintain honor. Men who are seen as dishonorable still pay a price because they have fewer resources and options. They're less likely to have allies when they need support. They can't meet their full potential at work. Their relationships are undependable and fleeting.

In short, the dishonorable man's weak social foundation translates into problems and conflicts. The woman who partners with him will inevitably inherit his troubles and be subject to his mistreatment.

It is a wise woman who chooses an honorable man. I knew a man who agreed to take in the teenage sister of his new wife when she suddenly found herself homeless. He certainly hadn't planned on providing for a demanding adolescent in the first years of his marriage. It would be costly and inconvenient, and his wife told him that she wouldn't bear a grudge if he refused. But he insisted on taking in the sister because, in his view, it was simply the right thing to do. From that moment on, his wife knew she would never face problems alone.

FOUR SIGNS HE'S STRIVING FOR HONOR

When it comes to honor, talk is cheap. Behavior is what counts. Here are four signs a man is striving to be honorable.

He is impeccable. He keeps his word. He takes pride in his work. He is honest. He accepts responsibility for his errors and he corrects them. He keeps his commitments. He's ethical even when ethics are inconvenient. He's the man who shows up early and stays late when there's a job to be done. He makes sure the little things are in order— tires properly inflated and bills paid on time—to prevent problems before they begin. He simply does what's right and principled.

He's resourceful. Dishonorable men take the easy road rather than face challenges. They abandon people; they quit jobs; they bend the rules in order to triumph over others in conflicts of interest. But the honorable man is above these actions. He's resourceful and he seeks solutions that benefit all concerned because he cares about the distant effect of his behavior.

He is honest. He doesn't possess the need or the desire to profit at the expense of others. He's stronger than that.

His honesty appears in small acts, like returning extra change when a cashier overcompensates him. He's also willing to face unpleasant truths, and he doesn't skirt responsibility or cover his tracks when he has erred or spoken an unkind word. When he must speak an unpleasant truth, he does so with compassion.

He is loyal. Anyone can be loyal when the sky is blue and the horizon is clear. Real loyalty shows itself in hard times when people need us most. Those are the moments when fearful or dishonorable men compound the pain of loved ones by vanishing. The honorable man doesn't let the team down. He has a consistent record of protecting the relationships, interests, and reputations of the people he cares for.

Like so many of the relationship-ready traits we've already discussed, no man will be flawlessly honorable every moment of his life. He will wrestle with ethical questions, and sometimes he will arrive at the wrong answer because that's the nature of ethical quandaries. The honorable man doesn't always get it right, but he always tries.

The Cost of Overlooking Values, Purpose, and Character

Words like "courtship" and "honor" may sound like anachronisms plucked from Elizabethan times, but they are powerful foundations for successful relationships. Years in the future, when the two of you face one of life's trials, you might be thankful you welcomed these old sentiments—especially as you watch other women pay the price of ignoring these fundamental qualities.

Consider Melissa, whose story is far too common. When she met Brandon, he seemed perfect on the outside. He was playful and energetic, and a bit of a hell-raiser. "I live in the moment," he would boast. She liked his devil-may-care approach to life, and so she ignored her friends' concerns about his seemingly unreliable character. "I don't know about him," her friends would say in a moment of candor. "Are you sure you can trust him?"

They moved in together after only six months, and—*surprise!*—she discovered his money problems after they signed a lease together. Brandon's definition of "living in the moment" had apparently meant ignoring credit card debt and skipping out on a prior lease with a roommate. Now his debts became hers. She was forced to pay his share of the rent so he could keep the collections agents at bay.

She remained with him because he promised to fix his financial affairs. Surprise again! He didn't change. He continued to squander money and disregard his obligations.

Her financial problems grew, thanks to his careless behavior, as did her unhappiness. She began to resent him. Unfortunately, she became pregnant and he became a deadbeat dad.

Melissa's future was forever hobbled by her encounter with Brandon. Her educational opportunities were foreclosed. Her professional aspirations were dashed. Worst of all, their daughter grew up without her father.

The warning signs of Brandon's low character were there from the beginning. She didn't allow time for courtship, so she didn't get to know him until she was already suffering because of his shortcomings.

She overlooked his habit of consuming more than he produced, both financially and emotionally. His "devil-may-care" approach to life amounted to little more than selfishness. He was flat-out dishonorable, and his man card was in tatters from the beginning. Melissa and their child paid a price for his weakness of character.

Partnering with a person of low character can be exhausting. You will be forced to make hard choices resulting from his unfulfilled obligations; you may find yourself lying to friends and family to cover for his embarrassing behavior; you might find yourself paying neglected bills; you may be forced to choose between him and other important relationships because others in your life reject him; you may even find yourself surrounded by his unsavory associates, whose behavior places you at even greater risk.

Melissa was never able to live up to her potential when she was with him. In addition to all the consternation he created, her decision-making abilities suffered under the distress, distraction, and fatigue he brought into her life.

Obviously, men of low character are different from those who simply lack a sense of purpose or shared values. But choosing a man who possesses all three traits—shared values, a sense of purpose, and a desire to be honorable—is the best insurance against the pain men like Brandon can cause.

The counterpoints to Melissa's sad, cautionary tale are all of the quiet, wonderful relationships built on values, purpose, and character. These couples are all around us. They don't make headlines; they're simply happy.

CHAPTER 8
APPRAISING HIS MENTAL HEALTH

By the time I met Amelia, her relationship with Charlie was slowly and painfully coming to an end. Though they were engaged to be married, he displayed little interest in being a fully functioning romantic partner. He had once been attentive and loving, but he was now sullen, irritable, and secretive.

Charlie had been drinking too heavily, sleeping poorly, and he was simply not taking care of himself physically. He cut off communication whenever Amelia approached him about saving the relationship. When she expressed concern about his well-being, as his friends and family had, he would dismissively tell her everything was fine and demand that she drop the subject. If pressed, he lashed out verbally. He had become so distant from her that he could not even tolerate her expressions of concern. This was a terrible way to start a marriage.

Amelia wondered what she could do to save their relationship, but it was beyond her control. Charlie was an otherwise good man who was suffering for reasons that he never explained. For all practical purposes, he was entirely unavailable for the relationship.

Relationship-ready men don't leave their partners in the dark. They are willing and able to commit. They desire the connection, and the women in their lives never have to worry about these men's commitment or intention.

For every Charlie in the world, there are countless relationship-ready men who take great care of themselves, their partners, and their relationships. The challenge is that those good men don't stand out because disorder always draws more attention than stability. Finding these healthy, capable men is going to require some tools. Here are this chapter's questions for appraising a man's mental health:

- Inspection Item 5: What role do substances and other forms of avoidance play in his life?
- Inspection Item 6: How does he handle male stoicism?
- Inspection Item 7: Does he value emotional insight?
- Inspection Item 8: Is he available?

The philosophical thread that runs through these questions is one of capacity for devotion. Mental health problems speak nothing of a person's character or worth as a human being. But *unresolved* mental or emotional difficulties deeply distract people from bringing their best and most capable selves to a relationship. With capacity for devotion in mind, let us begin with one of the most useful questions any man or woman can ask about a potential partner.

INSPECTION ITEM 5: WHAT ROLE DO SUBSTANCES AND OTHER FORMS OF AVOIDANCE PLAY IN HIS LIFE?

There's a phrase from the study of behaviorism that is of great importance to our discussion of good men: *experiential avoidance.* It refers to an inflexible pattern of avoiding painful thoughts, feelings, and memories, even when that avoidance is harmful.

Thoughts and feelings are like the weather. Sometimes they are stormy and beyond our control. If a person is fearful of something outside the skin, like elevators or airplanes, it's easy enough to simply avoid them. But when the feared experience comes from inside, like a traumatic memory or the thought of a lost love, we can't just walk away. We could be minding our own business one day, when—*Boom!*—something out of the blue evokes the thought or feeling we hoped to never encounter. Perhaps you have noticed that the more you try *not* to think of something, the stronger the thoughts become.

Want to try an experiment? Quick! Don't think of a monkey. Now try really, *really* hard not to think of a monkey. If you're mind works like mine, you can distract yourself from the thought of monkeys by singing *Jingle Bells* or counting backward, but now those imaginary monkeys are making us behave oddly. And we're not fooling anybody. We know we're trying to avoid the thought of monkeys. It's called *thought suppression*, and it tends to backfire. The harder we work to avoid imaginary monkeys, the more influence they have over us.

That's why people turn to destructive habits like substance abuse, compulsive sex, or needless shopping, just for the diversion and relief it provides. Those quick-relief behaviors turn off the painful thoughts and feelings, but only for a little while. When the thoughts and feelings return, so does the craving for the avoidant behavior. Experiential avoidance can become a vicious cycle in which a person works increasingly hard to avoid thoughts, feelings, and memories.

Here's another term from behaviorism: *negative reinforcement*. Many people think that term refers to punishment, but actually it refers to a kind of reward. When we do something to ease distress, the absence of pain serves as the prize. For example, if alcohol blunts a traumatic memory, then alcohol has provided negative reinforcement, and the person is likely to drink again in order to achieve the same effect. People tend to keep doing what reduces pain.

Why does this matter in a conversation about good men? Because a man's willingness to sit with discomfort increases his effectiveness, which as we've seen, is a crucial ingredient in his relationship readiness.

We've seen how men use experiential avoidance differently than women and how that can sometimes be useful. Think back, if you will, to the experiment in which men and women were shown disturbing pictures. Because men are generally trained to avoid emotions, they more easily tuned out the disturbing imagery.

That's the upside of experiential avoidance. The downside is its awful destructiveness when it becomes an inflexible, automatic response to emotional discomfort.

Impulsiveness is one of the particularly destructive, relationship-wrecking aspects of experiential avoidance (Berghoff et al. 2012). I'm not necessarily talking about rash behavior, like spontaneously hopping a junket to Vegas and spending the mortgage money, but rather decisions driven by the desire for immediate gratification rather than long-term considerations.

Think of the man who gets drunk at family gatherings in order to avoid tension with relatives. The goal of such an impulsive decision is to avoid uncomfortable family exchanges. It works, for a little while. For a short time, he gets to replace family tension with a warm, tipsy feeling. (The mind doesn't consider the next day's fallout when it devises such plans.) Shortsighted and strange though it may be, the speck of pain relief he gets from avoiding tension with the in-laws increases the likelihood he will get drunk around family again. That's the effect of negative reinforcement.

Decisions like those often have their roots in men's emotional training. I can't stress it enough: stoicism is a real puzzle for men. Each of us has to figure out when it is useful and when it is harmful. But wherever a man falls on the wide spectrum that is male stoicism, relationship-ready men don't give in to life-altering experiential avoidance.

You've probably already surmised that one of the most common and destructive forms of experiential avoidance among men is substance abuse.

Does He Have a Substance Abuse Problem?

Partnering with someone caught in the throes of substance abuse can be a nightmare. Drugs and alcohol ruin careers and families. They can destroy bank accounts and retirement plans. They can permanently damage bodies and minds.

I don't wish to overstate the case. Most people who use substances do so wisely and in moderation, but the man who lacks restraint is quite simply unprepared to be a reliable partner in an intimate relationship. (And if you'll pardon the repetition, marijuana can destroy relationships just like harder substances.)

The reality of a person's addiction may not show up until his life begins to fall apart, at which point the desire to avoid the ugly truth can propel a substance's destructive force even further. Even an otherwise honest person can develop the skills of a ninja when it comes to hiding substance abuse, so here are a few tips to help you see past drug-fueled subterfuge. He might be addicted if you find yourself...

Arguing with him about substances. The sober partner will at some point want to discuss the addicted partner's intemperance, while the addicted partner assiduously works to avoid the topic. Conflict ensues, with plenty of rationalization, indignation, and counter-accusations. Sometimes the topic of the argument *is* his unwillingness to discuss it.

Making excuses for him. Partners of addicts will frequently find themselves making excuses to friends, family, and coworkers. They find themselves defending their partner's odd behavior, rude manner, broken promises, and instability.

Complaining that getting high or drunk is all he wants to do with you. Addicts often find it impossible to have fun without being in an altered state. The sober partner will find him- or herself lobbying to take a break from getting drunk or high.

Avoiding friends and family to escape embarrassment. The sober partner frequently co-opts the shame experienced by an addicted partner, and may even feel compelled to participate in denial by avoiding friends and loved ones who might call attention to the problem.

Many addicts refuse to discuss their addiction. A person caught in the illness almost always avoids the topic. Addiction is layered with shame and anxiety that leads many otherwise honest people to conceal their troubles, or at least to try.

Eventually, their behaviors become hard to ignore—odd behavior changes, secrecy, health changes, habit changes, defensiveness, dismissiveness, manipulativeness, unlikely or peculiar stories and explanations, failure to meet responsibilities, and the warning sign that's most easily overlooked: the sober partner's intuition that something isn't right.

I've seen couples waste years limping along, refusing to acknowledge substance abuse. Both parties suffer immensely. The sober partners worry about the health and safety of their addicted loved one, and so they go along with subterfuge and denial because doing so is easier than exposing the truth and upending their lives. Meanwhile, they feel hopeless, embarrassed, deceived, and isolated.

Addicted partners also become well-practiced at reassurance and diversion. Don't fall for it. Heed the warning signs and insist on nothing less than honesty. The only meaningful response to addiction is to bring it into the light and get treatment.

It's a different story once he's clean and sober. People in recovery often develop amazing relationship skills and make ideal partners because the work involved in substance abuse treatment can lead to tremendous insightfulness and emotional resourcefulness.

How can you know if recovery is going well? For starters, the secrets, omissions, and manipulativeness will disappear. You'll know he is serious about recovery when he successfully navigates challenges and emotional difficulties without turning to substances. He will have built new circles of social support and jettisoned old acquaintances who fed his addiction. He will take care of his body and mind so he doesn't become overwhelmed and succumb to his old habits.

Across cultures, men are more prone to alcoholism and other drugs than women, and I have no doubt the distinction follows the different ways which men and women are trained to handle emotion. Men who turn to alcohol rather than address difficulties are more likely to be fearful of expressing "weak" negative emotions (Green and Addis 2012). These men often believe emotions like sadness, fear, or guilt are intolerable and dangerous, and they must be pushed away. An altered state of mind efficiently relieves the burden.

Substance abuse is often the manifestation of manly stoicism handled poorly, which brings us to our next question in the 12-point man inspection.

INSPECTION ITEM 6: HOW DOES HE HANDLE MALE STOICISM?

Stoicism is the tendency to endure hardship without complaint or emotional display. Research has shown it to be a very real and quantifiable part of the male psyche.

For example, one pair of researchers (Pierce and Kirkpatrick 1992) showed men and women videos of rats, mice, and roller-coaster rides meant to evoke fear. They also administered a survey asking the participants to rate their fear of situations such as heights, public speaking, and enclosed spaces. They were attempting to measure the participants' self-reported level of fear.

They then administered the same procedure to a different group. This time the researchers fibbed, warning participants they could measure fear by monitoring their pulse. In other words, they led the subjects to believe there would be no way to hide their fear, whereas subjects in the first condition had nothing preventing them from lying about the intensity of their fear.

Women's scores remained roughly the same between the two conditions, suggesting they probably answered honestly both times. But not the men. Their scores rose in the second condition, meaning they hid their fear when they thought they weren't being measured. They were more honest when they believed the researchers could see through their brave facade.

Although we men downplay our fear, we also appear to be less fearful in certain situations than women. That's probably due to both socialization and genetics.

While both genders are equally fearful of things like bodily injury or enclosed spaces, boys as young as nine years old report less anxiety over more benign objects like dogs or mice (McLean and Anderson 2009). Women also report the fear of public places more often than men.

The influence that gender has on fear is complex, thanks to hormonal effects on anxiety. Men are more likely to experience anxiety when their autonomic system is activated during challenge (like navigating a dangerous situation); women are more likely to experience anxiety when they are at rest.

In other words, men are less likely to experience feelings like fear or anxiety unless there's an imminent threat to physical safety. Women appear to be more sensitive to abstract threats, probably because women are more likely to ruminate or overestimate the probability of danger. McLean and Anderson showed that girls even begin experiencing more negative feelings than boys as early as age two. Another way to say it is that women are less reactively fearful than men, but have a higher baseline of anxiety during calm times.

Does this mean men are happier than women? Not at all. It simply means men and women, in general, have different biological predispositions for anxiety. Neither is superior because each serves a purpose. Add the fact that most boys are taught to be brave and face challenges aggressively, and you have two genders with quite different experiences of fear and anxiety.

Like any other human quality, male stoicism has advantages and drawbacks. On one hand, the ability to suppress emotions has been tied to psychological problems like anxiety, depression, and substance abuse. On the other, emotional suppression has also been tied to psychological wellbeing, especially when accompanied by positively reframing challenges (Karekla and Panayiotou 2011). There are other advantages, too:

- Stoicism helps us avoid ruminating on difficulties.
- It keeps us focused on goals.
- Because men's bodies don't stay anxious for long, our minds are able to recover from setbacks and disagreements quickly.
- Stoicism gives us a measure of insulation from life's harshness because we are trained to turn away from pain.

Male stoicism also prevents us from having emotional outbursts that feed on themselves and grow in intensity. Psychologists once believed that angry catharsis (yelling, punching pillows, and so forth) was healthy, and "bottling it up" was unhealthy.

Ancient male sensibility knows better. Cathartic expressions of anger don't reduce anger, they increase it (Bushman 2002). My manly grandfather could have told us that because men have known this for eons. That's why respectable men teach boys to manage their annoyance and hostility.

For as useful as it is, male stoicism has a few disadvantages in romance:

- It can interfere with us putting words to emotions and challenges, sometimes reducing our effectiveness.
- It leads us to replace "weak" emotions like sadness with "strong" emotions like anger.
- It compels us to withdraw and isolate rather than seeking help when we're worried, sad, or hurt.

Stoicism is truly the two-edged sword of male mental health. It is both wonderfully useful and awfully destructive. Men who are overly stoic are no fun to be around because they're prone to emotional problems, and they're tough to communicate with. Men who aren't stoic enough can be equally difficult to endure when they are helpless and histrionic.

So what's the right amount of stoicism for a man? It depends on the man. Couples argue over this routinely, though they are sometimes unaware they're quarreling over stoicism. More often, they think they're arguing over the time he spends on video games, or exercise, or other diversions.

Let's talk about those diversions.

We all need a break sometimes, and men in particular need a break from the stoicism balancing act. While experiential avoidance damages a person's ability to function, healthy diversion enhances it by giving the mind a chance to process emotion and recuperate.

Naturally, couples sometimes disagree about the amount of recuperative time he spends zapping zombies at a game console or doing preacher curls at the gym. I can't define the right amount of recuperation for any particular man. Instead, I can tell you that relationship-ready men take two important precautions to prevent stoicism from running rampant.

First, good men seek balance in all matters, including useful stoicism and the ability to honestly approach uncomfortable emotions like sadness, fear, and guilt. A *real* man possesses the emotional versatility to wrestle bears *and* have a heartfelt conversation with the woman he loves.

Second, good men use diversions intelligently and unapologetically. Yes, I said *unapologetically*. Though we rarely discuss it, the life of a good man involves a tremendous amount of emotional management. He has no reason to bear shame for occasionally escaping when his diversions serve to increase his emotional effectiveness.

APPRECIATING MALE STOICISM

The word "stoicism" seems to have a negative undertone. Those who devalue it erroneously equate it with being overly individualistic, emotionally detached, uncaring. That's unfortunate, because male stoicism can actually make a man a better partner— one who's adept at keeping problems in perspective, solving them, and moving on.

Stoicism makes him a less effective partner when it *prevents* him from solving problems with you as a team. Men with a slavish sensibility toward fortitude sometimes drive their partners crazy with emotional stonewalling. When confronted with a legitimate need to discuss the relationship, these men can become dismissive, irritable, angry, or avoidant. The stoicism ninja uses clever diversions like humor in his attempts to manipulate you into ignoring his problem.

These men deserve compassion because they often feel a great deal of shame and trepidation about their emotional experiences. Regardless, they leave you with a decision to make: is his manifestation of stoicism what you seek in a partner? A man who refuses to address problems leaves them for his partner to solve. Only you can decide how much silence is acceptable.

And here's the question each man faces: *Is stoicism serving my relationship well, or is it interfering with my willingness and ability to communicate with my partner?* Even if the answer is slow in coming, the relationship-ready man is at least willing to face the question.

I think few women understand how challenging it is for men to balance fortitude and emotional openness. We are punished for expressing our emotions, and we are punished for *not* expressing them. Balancing the pressure to be stoic against the expectation to communicate effectively is one of the most fundamental struggles for men.

INSPECTION ITEM 7: DOES HE VALUE EMOTIONAL INSIGHT?

Men who succeed in relationships have a sense of their own history and its effect on their behavior. Such was not the case with Ruben. His relationship with Nicole was governed by his jealousy and insecurity.

They had been dating a short time when small signs of the green-eyed monster began to creep in. It started with small behaviors like playfully quizzing her about her whereabouts and her friendships, or teasing that she belonged to him whenever other men were nearby. At first, she found it to be a charming indication of his affection for her, but it didn't remain charming for long.

His insecurity increased as the relationship matured and they discussed buying a house and starting a family. The previously playful quizzing began to resemble interrogation and monitoring. She once found him inspecting her cell phone to see if she had been communicating with other men.

He also began the particularly troubling habit of disparaging her friends and family. He increasingly disapproved of her time with them, as if to separate her from people who cared about her.

Ruben was never abusive or violent. He was simply quick to become angry and suspicious. He also increasingly retreated into using marijuana. Their arguments were always the same. He would accuse her of being interested in other men, and she would try to defend herself. It was miserable for both of them.

Unsurprisingly, the relationship didn't last. In retrospect, Nicole recognized what she couldn't see when she was in the midst of it. (Isn't that always the way?) She realized that their repetitive arguments neglected the real issue, Ruben's insecurity. Whenever she raised the subject, he masterfully deflected and focused the conversation on her shortcomings. "I wouldn't be jealous if *you* didn't flirt with every guy you met," he would say in his most wounded affectation.

Now, in hindsight, she speculated that behind his jealousy was the fear of being abandoned, and behind his refusal to discuss it was a lifelong aversion to introspection.

He came by his insecurity honestly. Both of his parents had been cold and distant figures. His mother had a volatile temper and had withdrawn her love when she was angry. Ruben never knew where he stood with her while growing up. Did she love him or not? He carried that insecurity into all of his relationships with women.

His father, while more emotionally consistent than his mother, prided himself on machismo and was quick to mock Ruben if he showed any kind of weakness or vulnerability. He once laughed when eleven-year-old Ruben came home crying from a pickup football game. His father mocked any show of feelings as "girly," and so Ruben naturally learned to quash any impulse to discuss feelings with the one parent who, though cold, was at least reliably present for him.

Perhaps it is no coincidence Ruben's father was a lifelong alcoholic. He probably used alcohol to manage disappointment and sadness in the same way Ruben used pot.

Ruben's parents not only failed to teach him how to be introspective, they actively discouraged it. They left him with a mountain of self-doubt, fear of abandonment, and few tools for managing his own emotions. Ruben's damaged view of himself, and his insecure view of women, was a normal reaction to an abnormal upbringing.

But we can only blame his parents up to a point. Ruben was now an adult and making his own choices, and he chose to remain mired in his miserable and ineffective patterns. His insecurity grew with each failed relationship, and rather than looking inward, he placed the blame on women. To his mind, *all* women—even Nicole—had the potential to be cruel and undependable. He had to protect himself.

Examining these forces within himself would have meant acknowledging what he regarded as "weak" emotions like insecurity and sadness. Instead, he turned those weak emotions into "strong" emotions like jealousy and anger. He was acting just like his parents.

Ruben chose to turn away from discomfort rather than to grow. Ironically, acting "strong" was a fear-driven behavior. We can only hope he eventually realized there was a better way to go through life.

Nicole had given Ruben plenty of chances to change. She had tried talking to him about his insecurity during calm moments when he might be receptive. She had asked him to attend couple's therapy with her. She tried giving him space. She tried every avenue she could think of to improve their communication. Sadly, he stonewalled her at every turn.

Nicole moved on, which was probably a wise decision. Ruben was generally a decent guy who was ill-suited for relationships because he was utterly unwilling to examine his own destructive patterns. Relationships simply cannot function under an allegiance to such ruinous habits.

Ruben is not in the majority. Most men are willing to look inward. Introspection can be uncomfortable, and we don't always want to talk about it, but trustworthy men don't let damaging patterns fester and grow. They are strong enough to examine themselves and accept responsibility for their effects on others.

One of the most uplifting qualities a relationship-ready man possesses is curiosity about matters of emotion and communication. I knew a man whose wife was becoming increasingly unhappy because he was spending so much time away from home at work and with hobbies. And because he wasn't home when she was fuming over the responsibilities he left her with, he didn't realize she was angry.

Curiosity is the foundation of insight. When she finally told him that she was becoming resentful, he went beyond merely agreeing to spend more time at home. He wanted to know how long she had been unhappy, and why he hadn't realized how angry she was becoming. They discovered important communication deficits—some on his end, and some on hers—that they would not have uncovered had he responded with defensiveness rather than openness and curiosity.

Let's not ignore reality. Most men don't want to dwell in lengthy, emotional, relationship dialogue. That even includes the guy who's writing this book. The question is not whether he will converse with you for hours in the middle of the night, unless that's of special import to you. Rather, it is whether he is willing to examine, acknowledge, and accept responsibility for his own motivations and behaviors.

(If you'll permit me a brief tangent, knowing when to *stop* discussing relationship dynamics is also a vital skill. People in healthy relationships don't generally dissect every dynamic and interaction, unless they both find the topic particularly intriguing. For any given couple, there is a point of diminishing returns at which it is best to get on with the business of enjoying life. The inability to step away from exhausting relationship discourse is often the sign of an unresolved problem, the true nature of which neither side is recognizing.)

There's another consideration to make when assessing his level of self-knowledge. Male emotional insight sometimes lags behind women. Some of us, like Ruben, have been trained to avoid it altogether. Sometimes we require patience. If a man is curious and open, then he is growing.

INSPECTION ITEM 8: IS HE AVAILABLE?

Most of us have known people who wasted years pining for someone who had no intention of settling down. Maybe they devoted themselves to someone whose first love was alcohol, or work, or the single life. Maybe they dated someone who was clearly using them for sex. Maybe they gave second, third, and fourth chances to a serial cheater. Perhaps they even made the mistake of being the "other man" or "other woman."

(Here's a quick tip regarding fidelity. If a man is cheating on someone else when he begins wooing you, then he'll be willing to cheat on you someday.)

A woman once complained to me that the man she was interested in was, by his own report, "too insecure and complicated" to make a commitment. She occupied only a small part of his life, and the rest he kept hidden from her. By the time she discussed it with me, he hadn't spoken to her for several weeks. She wanted to know how to revive the relationship. You might be thinking, as I did, *there was no relationship to revive*.

I'm not opposed to fantasies. I've long daydreamed about owning a Lamborghini. Sometimes I catch myself planning how I will store the car, and what tools I'll need to maintain it. (It's a white 1986 Countach, by the way.) Yes, my mind loses track of reality sometimes.

The fantasy is fun, and it is only a hindrance if I put my life on hold for it. The truth is, even when I can one day afford it I probably won't own one. It's not the car for me. I'm a pickup-truck kind of guy, so I won't forego a solid vehicle while I'm waiting for my Lamborghini. Life is too short.

A man who is ready for a relationship generally isn't complicated, and he doesn't require a woman to fantasize about his availability. He knows what he wants in life and he pursues it. He doesn't partition off his life or disappear into experiential avoidance. He certainly doesn't keep a girlfriend on the side, because he's serious about commitment. If there are complications interfering with his relationship goals, he's dealing with them honestly and efficiently so he can have what he wants: *you*.

In chapter 10, we'll look at two kinds of men to avoid at all costs. We'll also uncover the mental and emotional errors that cause women to pursue those cads. For now, I'll simply beseech you not to abide fantasy when you are assessing a man's level of commitment. Listen to the facts.

What's the best way to know if he's available and ready to commit? Ask him, then be honest with yourself about his answer and his behavior. During your all-important courtship, is he becoming emotionally closer to you, or is he retreating, partitioning, and avoiding?

Remember also that friends and family sometimes have the clearer view of him than you do. Don't waste time on Mr. Unavailable when Mr. Right is out there searching for you.

What About Ultimatums?

We've seen it in the movies, and sometimes in real life. She wants a commitment, but he doesn't, so she issues the relationship ultimatum: marry me or we're done.

No one likes to be on the receiving end of an ultimatum. But at the same time, you have a right to know where you stand. It is unfair for a man, or a woman, to force a partner to put life on hold while he or she struggles to make a decision. What's a person to do when a partner won't commit?

Relationship ultimatums are counterproductive when framed with coercion that leaves the recipient with two unpleasant choices: either comply with my demand and be resentful, or disobey and be punished. Here are a few examples of poorly planned and counterproductive ultimatums:

- "If you don't start cleaning the kitchen, then I'm going to stop cooking."
- "Start talking to me more, or the sex ends."
- "Propose to me by Christmas, or I'll find someone who will."

Each one of those ultimatums starts with a legitimate concern: I need help in the kitchen; I want better communication; I want to get married. The problem is one of presentation. It's angry and threatening. It forces the recipient into a submissive or defensive posture. And it fails to establish whether the person is prepared or able to meet the demand. The worst part about ultimatums is that sometimes the recipient desires the same outcome as the person issuing the demand, but the ultimatum feels so aggressive it fore-closes that mutual desire.

Although ultimatums can backfire, you have every right to know where you stand, and every right to reject someone who doesn't share your willingness to commit to the level you desire. Instead of issuing coercive ultimatums that diminish options, consider phrasing your concern in a way that creates options.

Here's the same propose-to-me-by-Christmas ultimatum phrased in a way that empowers the recipient rather than corner-ing him: "I would like to be married to you. It's important to me. I know you are reluctant, and I respect your feelings. Still, I need to move forward in life. If, by the end of the year, you don't share my desire to be married then I will be sad, but I will know it is time to move on."

This phrasing serves the same purpose as an ultimatum. It tells him you need answers, but does so without stealing his power or dignity. It focuses on the desire for success rather than the threat of punishment. A respectable man will respond wisely and com-passionately, even if the answer is no.

The Cost of Overlooking His Unwillingness to Commit

The heart is shortsighted. The mind will collude with it, if you're not careful, and drag you into a fantasy world. Your job is to keep an eye on both of these troublemakers.

Don't make the same mistake as Lillian, a woman I knew. She pursued a man who was ambivalent about the relationship from the beginning. While he repeatedly professed his love and commitment to her, he routinely treated the relationship as a low priority. For example, she would make plans based on his promises, only to find those plans dashed at the last moment when he cancelled in favor of an online video game tournament or an alcohol-fueled camping trip with his buddies.

The conflicting messages were cruel, and they took a toll on her. She frequently found herself covering for his broken commitments. She was embarrassed whenever he abandoned their plans with friends and family. She lost sleep worrying about his whereabouts when he was gone. She lost weight because the anxiety ruined her appetite.

She wanted to build a family in a loving and equitable relationship. Instead, she found herself lost in a morass of worry and supervision. By the time she finally acknowledged his refusal to commit she had sacrificed two years and foregone untold opportunities with other men who might have cherished her.

Hers was precisely the type of predicament that arises with a partner who is in poor mental health and who is avoiding solutions. Whether he lacks the willingness or the capacity to commit, the result is the same.

A good, relationship-ready man possesses the mental tools to succeed in a relationship. He's searching for you, and he's capable of adding more to your life than he takes, so be honest with yourself when you assess these qualities in a man. Don't waste time fantasizing about someone who lacks the capacity or the desire to commit.

Chapter 9
Evaluating His
Emotional Maturity

There are countless men who possess high character, values similar to yours, and the desire to be in a committed relationship. It is all for naught if he lacks the basic emotional skills necessary to be a fully functioning partner. Here are the four remaining questions in our 12-point man inspection:

- Inspection Item 9: How does he handle bad moods and bad days?
- Inspection Item 10: Does he possess reliable coping skills?
- Inspection Item 11: How does he treat others?
  ...and one of the most serious questions in this book:
- Inspection Item 12: How does he treat you?

The philosophical thread that runs through these questions is one of relationship skills. By definition, an emotionally mature person possesses certain basic skills for navigating relationships and handling problems. His skillset will reveal itself in the way he interacts with you and with others.

At the end of chapter 8, we discussed the fantasy of the unavailable man who might magically become a committed partner. Well, fantasizing is also a hazard where relationship shortcomings are concerned. This is yet another mistake driven by optimism. It is tempting to believe we are capable of conquering any challenge, including the emotional shortcomings of others. Beware the fantasy that he'll outgrow those troubling little warning signs. Perhaps he will, but not through the power of love. It will require resourcefulness, effort, and maturity on his part.

I think the desire to avoid an unhappy breakup is the main reason we overlook emotional immaturity in a prospective mate. Why rock the boat if he's nice, and devoted, and has a sunny personality? What could possibly go wrong in the future?

Just this: life will get tough at some point, and a shiny personality isn't enough to overcome adversity. The good, relationship-ready man possesses the skills to navigate rough waters. These four questions will help you predict how steady and skillful he'll be during life's challenges.

We'll start with a question every couple faces sooner or later.

INSPECTION ITEM 9: HOW DOES HE HANDLE BAD MOODS AND BAD DAYS?

His inauspicious day will arrive eventually. It's the day when he has a job interview and his car won't start, or the network is down while he's working on a deadline. Maybe his water heater is leaking, his car key broke off in his ignition, and he discovered his fly had been open during a two-hour meeting with his boss.

How will he behave? Will he become a sullen, pouting mess that you must somehow put back together? Will he be immobilized with ineffective coping skills? Or will he handle it with the resourcefulness of Batman and the resilience of John Wayne?

Men who actively tackle their problems are not only more effective; they are healthier. Greenberg and colleagues (2009) found that men who ineffectually ruminate or avoid problems are more prone to depression than men who take a problem-solving approach. Depression, in turn, impairs initiative and effectiveness. It's an ugly cycle.

The Greenberg study certainly isn't suggesting there's something wrong with emotional expression. Complaining can be healthy, up to a point. But while everyone needs to vent occasionally, healthy and effective men take action at some point. They don't perceive themselves as powerless against life's setbacks.

Depression is often intertwined with ineffective problem-solving in men. We men are especially prone to depression when we handle setbacks with angry behaviors like being hyper-critical of others, when we isolate to avoid appearing weak, when we view depression as "a women's condition," or when we use risky behaviors like drug abuse to escape emotional distress (Oliffe et al. 2012).

Depression-prone men sometimes view maladaptive and ineffective strategies as more acceptable to society. For example, one young man in the study explained why he withdrew when he was upset rather than taking a problem-solving approach: "I mean it's hard to show emotion…as a guy I can't explain it…like you don't show emotion in front of your friends." Another explained, "Men are supposed to prove their worth to the group…you're not supposed to seem like a liability…and then being depressed looks like a major liability, and not the person you'd want to go out with…"

Not all the men in the study withdrew when they were struggling. Some turned their sadness to anger, or dissociated from emotion through risky behavior. These men expressed similar motivations. Stonewalling is easier and more accepted than expressing vulnerability. Though these men may have understandable reasons for insulating themselves from feelings of vulnerability, it exacts a cost in relationships.

Good, relationship-ready men are problem solvers. What signs are indicative of a man's emotional resourcefulness? In my clinical experience, the two most reliable indicators are good self-care and a reliable support system. Resourceful, problem-solving men might be caught flat-footed once in a while, but they're rarely caught without these solid resources from which to draw strength.

GOOD SELF-CARE

Self-care is the ability to tend to one's own body and mind without being prompted, and before needs become critical. You can be sure that John Wayne and Batman knew the value of proper sleep, diet, and exercise. They surely knew to address physical and mental needs before they became unmanageable. Poor self-care contributes to precisely the kinds of mood and coping difficulties that can damage relationships, particularly depression.

Depression damages men's health (Atlantis et al. 2011). Depressed men suffer low muscle strength, cardiovascular disease, high blood pressure, and even urinary tract problems. They are likelier than nondepressed men to be smokers, have a poor diet, be unmarried, and suffer from anxiety and insomnia.

So which comes first, depression or poor self-care?

Depression and physical health are intimately connected, and they are a two-way street. A man can become depressed simply by *failing* to take care of himself, and he can help himself recover by improving his routines. In other words, a man's level of self-care can be the cause or the effect, and it can be a symptom or the cure. For men in particular, avoiding conditions like depression means starting from the ground up by taking good care of ourselves.

We all eventually face this question: Which comes first—our problems or the manner in which we manage our lives? For example, smoking cigarettes may be an attempt to regulate low mood among people who are especially sensitive to nicotine's short-term mood-enhancing effect. At the same time, those nicotine-sensitive people are more prone to its long-term increase in risk of depression (Boden, Fergusson, and Horwood 2010).

Self-care often boils down to avoiding the long-term cost of a short-term pleasure, whether it's cigarettes, cookies, or too much TV. Depression typically improves when these costly, short-term strategies are replaced with healthy, long-term strategies. Unfortunately, avoiding short-term temptations is exhausting when a person is depressed. Smart men keep themselves healthy *before* they fall into the quicksand of poor self-care. That's why you never see Batman or John Wayne drowning their sorrows in a box of double-fudge cookies.

Young men are particularly prone to lifestyle choices that chip away at mental and physical health. I'm not just talking about alcohol and fast cars. Young men are prone to too much caffeine, too much sugar, too much alcohol, poor sleep habits and a generally awful diet.

The relationship-ready man has a self-care regimen. He wants to function at full capacity, not merely to please others, but for himself. While this may all seem obvious from a distance, some men neglect these basics. They don't give themselves the same loving attention they would give to their car.

Self-neglect harms relationships, especially when the chips are down and a man has few reserves to fall back on. Like a well-maintained car, a well-maintained man will be ready to go when you need him instead of sputtering along, eventually leaving you stranded on the side of the road.

RELIABLE SUPPORT SYSTEM

Healthy men usually maintain a network of other stand-up guys who help them maintain perspective. There's usually some good-nature busting of chops involved, but believe it or not, men do offer each other emotional support.

Plenty of men are independent by nature. They prefer to handle matters on their own. But there's a difference between temporarily retreating, and getting sucked into a downward spiral of social withdrawal and experiential avoidance.

The man who uses isolation constructively soon resurfaces with a solution in hand and in better condition than when he left. He's not hungover, or marinating in his anger and misery, or puzzling over how to rebuild relationships he damaged when he told the world to slag off before disappearing into a black hole of self-pity.

Even healthy men who rely on periodic isolation keep a support system of mentors, friends, and other smart men. Emotional support among men obviously doesn't always resemble emotional support among women. It may appear in short bursts during a break in jujitsu class, or while rock climbing, or between frames on bowling night. There might even be a few beers involved.

Whatever the form, it is just as vital for men to keep a network of other decent men as it is for women to keep friends outside the relationship. That group must include people who are willing to question our behavior and motives. Without it, neither partner is bringing their best self to the relationship because their emotional toolbox is missing a crucial tool for viewing themselves from another person's perspective.

You can tell a lot about a man by the people he chooses to surround himself with. If you find the conduct of his friends and associates to be admirable, then admirable behavior is probably important to him. Beware the man who hangs out with ne'er-do-wells and perpetual adolescents.

Good self-care and a reliable support system take work to maintain, and the wise woman offers a man space to do so. You might not always understand his rituals or his emotional supports, just as he might not understand yours. That's OK. Flawless understanding between women and men matters less than people think. Sometimes it's enough to know that your partner is doing what he needs to do to take care of himself.

You'll know if those practices are serving their purpose by the condition of his man card. If he's able to successfully manage bad moods and bad days—if he contributes more to the world and to your relationship than he consumes—then I encourage you to make allowances for his strange male ways.

Inspection Item 10: Does He Possess Reliable Coping Skills?

A grandmother once told me how her family vetted men who were interested in the young ladies of the family. Whenever a young woman was getting serious with a man, the fathers and uncles would take him golfing to find out how he reacted to stress. Since golf is a frustrating game, especially with the men of the family intentionally escalating the tension, they believed he would reveal his true character by the 18th hole.

Their logic was brilliant. Anyone can fake a favorable impression for a brief period of time, but it is tough to maintain a facade when you're tired and frustrated. Would the new suitor handle the aggravation with grace and humor? Would he sulk or get angry? Would he curse and throw his clubs into the lake? Time and pressure would reveal his temperament.

This family didn't want their daughters burdened by a partner's emotional deficits. They recognized the importance of reliable coping skills in a man.

What's in His Emotional Toolbox?

Each of us faces a choice when life throws a curveball. There's the problem-solving approach in which we strive to change situations and overcome hardships. Then there's the emotion-focused approach in which we strive to manage our feelings about problems. It's the difference between focusing outward on the matter at hand, or inward on ourselves. Or some combination of the two. People aren't so binary as to choose only one path—inward or outward—though they tend toward one response or the other.

While the emotion-focused approach rarely solves the external problem, it usually includes adaptive behaviors such as seeking social support or reframing our view of the situation. But taken too far, emotional management can turn into experiential avoidance.

For example, I knew a man who was unable to be present for his wife when her sister became ill, thanks to his excessively emotion-focused approach. He retreated into video games when his wife was distraught and overwhelmed with all of the family business she needed to attend to. He simply didn't have the emotional reserves to help her through distressing events, and so placed all of his energy toward managing his own emotions.

His was an emotion-focused solution in the extreme. Fortunately, he was willing to acknowledge his limitation after the crisis had resolved, and he began learning how to remain present the next time.

Relationship-ready men prefer to be useful. Skilled problem solvers who seek information, make plans, and take action end up healthier than people who rely on strategies such as avoidance, confrontation, wishful thinking, or focusing on keeping their emotions at bay (Penley, Tomaka, and Wiebe 2002). A man's problem-solving ability is a reflection of his overall well-being and his relationship readiness.

Effective coping means a man has the ability to handle *both* the situation and his emotions. Richard Lazarus (1993) has written about what he calls "planful problem solving," and it sounds like the problem-cracking blueprint for any relationship-ready man. Here's what it involves:

- identifying the problem and its solution without succumbing to denial or avoidance
- making a plan and following it without succumbing to discouragement, constant reappraisals, or setbacks
- being able and willing to change course when the solution doesn't go according to plan

Lazarus says the most skillful efforts can lead to distress when they fail, and that's when a person needs the ability to fall back on emotion-focused strategies like seeking social support or practicing positive reappraisal. For example, they might say to themselves, *It was a tough experience, but I'm better for it.* Could there be any manlier response?

Al Seibert, in *The Survival Personality* (2010), wrote about several specific emotional tools leading to resiliency, including the willingness to accept life's unfairness, possessing a playful curiosity, being flexible in the face of life's challenges, and attempting to find the opportunity in misfortune.

In other words, a good man has a big ol' toolbox for managing both real-world obstacles and his own feelings.

You don't have to wait for jumbo-sized challenges like a family illness to size up his resilience. It will show up in little, daily interactions. Imagine, for example, he tries to take you to his favorite restaurant, only to discover it has been boarded up. His reaction will give you a little glimpse into his toolbox. If he responds with resilience, seizing the opportunity to discover something new and adventurous, then he's just shown a bit of emotional durability. Little assessment opportunities like that one arise regularly.

I'm not suggesting you dump him based on less-than-resilient reactions to small challenges. Some people handle big problems with more grace then small disappointments. The skilled emergency physician who struggles with minor interpersonal conflicts comes to mind. However, I am suggesting that a pattern of counterproductive responses to small challenges bears scrutiny. Pouting and tantrums get old quickly.

A full toolbox generally shows itself in a positive attitude toward adversity. In many of life's challenges, positivity is more valuable than a perfect response. Remember the golf test. The family wasn't concerned about a man's score. They were measuring his ability to handle bad moods and bad days since life offers a generous supply of each.

Inspection Item 11. Is He Kind to Others?

This question is more than merely "is he a nice guy?" It has little to do with generosity or politeness because those behaviors can be misleading. Even the worst among us can feign warmth. Psychopaths and criminals are the most accommodating people in the world, when it suits them.

Kindness means he possesses a connection to others. He can detect their struggles and lessen the burden, rather than acting indifferently or, worse, capitalizing on other people's vulnerabilities. Like his problem-solving ability, his consideration appears in small encounters. For example, he doesn't rush to the front of the line when a cashier opens a new lane at the grocery store. He defers to those who have been waiting longer, and he does so out of empathy. The small advantage he would gain from jumping to the front of the line would be outweighed by the uncomfortable knowledge that he had treated others disrespectfully.

Kindheartedness doesn't mean he's a pushover. The virtuous man expects others to provide the same consideration he offers, and he's willing to draw the line rather than tolerate maltreatment.

So how does all this fit into our relationship-readiness inspection? His small behaviors in the world provide a reasonable estimate of your future with him. If a man is unkind early in the relationship then it's a safe bet he will only get worse with time. (Kind people sometimes don't know how to recognize unkind behavior. Don't worry if that's you. I'll give you some guidelines in our final inspection item.)

In my clinical experience, women are prone to two different types of mistakes when assessing a man's heart.

The first is what we might call "the illusion of false shelter." This happens early in relationships with men who treat their new girlfriends like queens, while at the same time they are rude to other people. This creates the illusion that the women in their lives rise above all others in importance.

The illusion of false shelter can also create a "you and me against the world" dynamic, fooling a couple into thinking they're closer than they really are. Intimacy through conflict works best in the movies. In real life, continual conflict with the world becomes rather a pain in the backside.

If he treats others poorly, then you can bet he will one day mistreat you, too. The icing on this miserable cake is the slow isolation his behavior will impose on you. His adversaries will one day become your own. Nobody likes a jerk, and they eventually tire of the jerk's significant other.

The second error runs in the opposite direction, keeping women away from good, relationship-ready men. We might call it "the illusion of false wimpiness."

Women sometimes confuse kindness with spinelessness. Good guys aren't willing to throw their weight around to win a woman's heart, and so their fortitude sometimes goes unnoticed. (Except to women who know what to look for!)

There are expensive trade-offs to partnering with a man who routinely allows himself to be exploited, not the least of which is his potential failure to defend loved ones. Most women are naturally and justifiably put off by what appears to be wimpiness.

But real wimpiness can be tough to distinguish from serene confidence. The wimp and the serenely confident man might respond identically to the jerk who kicks proverbial sand in his face, but for different reasons. The wimp walks away because he doesn't know how to defend himself while the confident man walks away because the conflict isn't worth the effort.

Unfortunately, you don't know how he's going to respond to a genuine transgression until you watch him in action. This is one more reason for a nice, long courtship. You'll eventually find out if your nice guy is willing to defend his values.

Most men will wear their best faces early in a relationship. Here are two tests to help you discern whether his kindness is genuine:

- How does he get his needs met?
- Is his presence a net benefit to others?

HOW DOES HE GET HIS NEEDS MET?

Sooner or later, we all need a little emotional support, some assistance, or maybe just some help moving a couch. The healthy man (or woman) gets those needs met through honest and forthright means.

There are people who haven't yet developed the ability to speak about their needs and accept help, and so they resort to coercion or manipulation. Both are relationship killers.

Such was the case with Randy, who briefly dated a woman named Elise. At first, he seemed like Elise's ideal man. He was friendly and funny. He made a wonderful first impression on her family and friends, bolstered by a lucrative career as an independent contractor in the tech field. His book of professional connections was impressive. He knew just whom to call for anything from leaky faucets to broken databases.

After they had been dating for a while, Randy noticed a text message from an ex-boyfriend on Elise's cell phone. This evidently troubled him, as he stewed on it for several days before discussing it with her. During that time, he indiscriminately complained about her to anyone who would listen. He even told mutual acquaintances that she had cheated on him. Eventually, the rumors reached Elise.

When she approached him about it, he answered with vague accusations that she had been dishonest. Elise didn't know what was talking about, or what had prompted his anger. As the conversation continued, his intensity escalated until he was demanding detailed answers to questions about her whereabouts and her past relationships. Finally, long into the argument, Randy revealed his knowledge of the ex-boyfriend's text message.

That text message had been an innocent, work-related inquiry, but Randy didn't believe it. After a long and painful night of arguing and defending herself, Elise was able to calm Randy down, though his suspicions lingered. It resurfaced anytime she received a text message in his presence.

It wasn't her last irrational argument with Randy. He developed a pattern of punishing her with the silent treatment whenever he was upset, and then interrogating and berating her when she attempted to reestablish communication.

The text-message incident was the first indication of Randy's maladaptive means of getting his needs met. Had he been able, the more constructive response would have been to admit he felt insecure about the relationship, ask Elise if he should be worried about the text message, and exercise the emotional fortitude to accept her answer.

Instead, his insecurity ruled the day, as it would a petulant child. He retreated into bitterness and paranoia. Instead of speaking to her directly, he started rumors. Instead of accepting her affection, he fearfully lashed out at her. Such ineffectiveness became his pattern with her.

He was always apologetic after his emotional tsunami receded, which was part of what kept Elise invested in him. At his core, he was a nice guy who was easily injured, but his self-soothing strategies were primitive and destructive. Eventually, though it saddened her to leave him, she was no longer willing to tolerate the emotional roller coaster.

A relationship-ready man is willing to acknowledge his needs. He uses the skills and strategies we've discussed to satisfy them:

- the insight to identify the problem he's facing
- the coping skills and communication tools to handle it constructively
- the resilience to recognize challenges as growth opportunities
- the desire and the ability to act honorably and impeccably, especially in the midst of emotional challenges

I knew a man who felt that his mother-in-law was exerting far too much negative influence over his children. He found her to be overly permissive when she babysat them, which he believed taught the children bad habits and led them to act in an entitled and bratty fashion. The mother-in-law was unwilling to alter her behavior, despite multiple requests from both parents.

As you can imagine, this situation could have caused family strife had he handled his annoyance poorly. But rather than becoming sarcastic, or passive-aggressive, or retreating, or otherwise responding counterproductively, he made sure he clearly understood the problem and then approached his wife during a calm moment. He explained that he wasn't willing to allow the situation to continue, and he was also concerned about the tension this might cause between his wife and her mother.

He proposed specific changes that lifted the burden of asking his wife to confront her mother, and he accepted the fact that transitioning to new arrangements with the children would take time. He was resolute, but he was also easygoing and empathetic about the problem. (If this example seems paternalistic, I'd recommend precisely the same approach to any woman who found herself in a similar position.)

After negotiating the details with his wife, the husband took the lead in arranging new babysitters so that the children would no longer be left alone with their grandmother. He also took responsibility for explaining the new arrangement to his mother-in-law.

Without rehashing his grievances, he explained that, of course, they wanted her to remain in the children's lives, but that he had decided on new babysitting arrangements. Not surprisingly, the grandmother was upset at first, but the father remained resolute. She realized that she would rather see the children on their parents' terms than not at all.

This father protected the interests of his family by constructively mitigating a harmful influence. He did so politely, and he did not back down in the face of resistance. He got his needs met in a healthy and forthright manner.

Is His Presence a Benefit to Others?

In any market-based economy there are net-tax providers and net-tax receivers. Everyone pays into the community till to some degree, even if it is merely through sales tax on a pack of cigarettes. And everyone benefits from those taxes, even if they're merely buying groceries that were delivered on public roads. The net-tax payers contribute more than they consume, while the net-tax receivers consume more than they produce.

This economic reality is a solid metaphor for life in general. Some people give more than they take, and no self-respecting man wants to be a net-receiver, literally or metaphorically.

Sometimes life forces us into the net-receiver category. That's no reflection of temperament or desire. But *choosing* to be a receiver rather than a provider is exploitation. It raises the question of character when a man elects to live off the efforts of others rather than pull his own weight.

Appearances can be deceiving, as they were with Randy. In many ways, his presence was a benefit to others. He was always willing to help out, and he was great at connecting people who could benefit from each other. If you needed a plumber, or a mechanic, or even a pot dealer, he probably knew one who would be happy to help.

In a different respect, he was a drain on his friends. For starters, he burdened them with complaints about Elise when he should have been speaking to her. He also put his friends in an awkward position by using them to communicate his dissatisfaction with Elise. That's manipulative. He wasn't merely receiving the benefit of his friendships in those moments, he was *taking* from them.

Even though he offered a lot in his good moments, Randy was a net-friendship receiver. A man's cost or benefit to others is a reliable gauge of his relationship-readiness for a couple of reasons.

First, he will one day treat you as you see him treating others. It is easy to overlook this character question because people treat each other wonderfully for the first few weeks or months of a relationship, but that kind deference doesn't last among people of low character or poor coping skills. Observing his effect on others is a wonderful way to catch a glimpse of your future with him after the honeymoon wears off.

One of my favorite character assessments is what we might call the "waiter test." You simply observe how he treats people he doesn't need to treat well, like a waiter, a subordinate at work, or a stranger on the subway. A man who is kindhearted and comfortable in his skin wouldn't dream of mistreating these people. If he does treat them poorly, I'd wager he will eventually treat *you* poorly.

The companion to the waiter test is the "boss test." How he handles disagreements with people who hold authority is just as telling as his interactions with those who don't. The good man handles conflict directly, constructively, and politely. Beware the man who goes behind his superiors' back, over their head, or passive-aggressively defies them. If he treats his superiors disrespectfully during conflict, there's no reason to think he'll treat you any better when tensions rise.

The second reason to pay close attention to his treatment of others has to do with his effect on your reputation. If he is a burden to others, then eventually *you* will become a burden by association. He won't be the only one who doesn't get invited to the holiday block party. You won't be invited, either.

In his dealings with others, the relationship-ready man is…

Flexible. He's able to adjust when events don't go according to plan. He's part of the solution, not part of the problem, and he meets disappointment with eventual good cheer.

Mature. He has ready access to the type of coping skills we have discussed. He is not entitled or bitter. He treats others as he would be treated.

Effective. He doesn't flounder ineffectually, as Randy did when he was worried about Elise's text message. He is direct, polite, and constructive, and he attends to the needs and interests of others because he knows resourcefulness involves win-win solutions.

This sort of confident and kindhearted man is particularly prone to creating the illusion of false wimpiness because he doesn't throw his weight around. But if he's flexible, mature, and effective, then he is hardly a wimp. And if his presence is a net benefit to others, then it might just be a net benefit to you as well.

INSPECTION ITEM 12. IS HE KIND TO YOU?

Have you ever heard someone say this about their relationship?
"When it's good, it's great."

That kind of sentiment makes me cringe because I've seen the inner workings of enough relationships to understand the real meaning:
Sometimes he treats me well, but it never lasts.

If I happen to be at a social gathering when I hear, "When it's good, it's great," then I smile and nod politely. But if I'm in my clinic, being a psychologist, I ask the next logical question: "Is he kind to you?" This is the most basic question in this book, and the most cryptic for some women. (Men have a similar struggle.)

Some people don't even know what it means to be with someone who is kindhearted because they have simply never experienced it, nor has it been modeled for them. If you haven't experienced kindness, allow me to suggest a way to begin thinking about it.

Kindness means he's empathetic and thoughtful. He's polite when he speaks to you. He's attentive to your needs. His behavior toward you is guided by compassion. He shares his thoughts with you, and he listens to yours with interest. He doesn't punish you for his rough day. Instead, he makes your day brighter and better.

The kindhearted man is never abusive, manipulative, or controlling. Like anyone, he might lose composure once in a while and say something hurtful, but he's quick to acknowledge his error and apologize. And this point is crucial: his slip-ups are not cyclical. He doesn't routinely become nasty or abusive, even if he says "baby, I'm sorry," each and every time.

Women who are accustomed to being treated poorly sometimes fail to recognize cyclical abuse or nastiness for what it is. They buy into the abusive man's line of worthless apologies and his empty promises to change in the future.

Sometimes people are aware they're being mistreated but they remain in unhealthy relationships because it seems better than the alternative. Even the thought of losing a bad relationship can be painful if it means

- becoming lonely;
- experiencing the fear of never again being loved;
- disrupting the lives of children;
- enduring the pain of splitting assets;
- finding new living arrangements;
- losing the monetary security or material comfort of the relationship;
- uprooting one's life and forfeiting predictability; and/or
- losing relationships with cherished in-laws and mutual friends.

Breaking up is hard, messy, and complicated even when it is the best option. Cruel men can make breakups even more taxing, which is one more reason to find kindhearted men and rule out the mean-spirited schlubs of the world.

If the notion of being with a kindhearted man is new to you—and there's no shame in that—then please study this section until the idea sinks in. Make it part of your worldview, even if it feels unnatural to believe men can and should treat you well. I'd offer the same advice to men who are unaccustomed to believing in the kindness of women.

Let's look at two more habits of the kindhearted man: he wants to be important to you, and he carefully maintains his relationships.

A Good Man Wants to Be Important to You

I wrote in *The Woman's Guide to How Men Think* about a young man I once saw standing on his motorcycle while riding past a group of young women. Naturally, he wrecked his bike. And naturally, he laughed it off because he was trying to win their affections.

Perilous bravado is a young man's game. (Think twice if a forty-five-year-old man tries to win your heart with such reckless shenanigans.) As silly as it may seem, bravado comes from the male desire to be important to women. Luckily for all concerned, we men refine our methods with age, even if the compulsion remains.

We want to matter to women, regardless of our age. We want to be needed, and good men steer that desire toward kindness, as opposed to people who make themselves necessary by fabricating an unhealthy power dynamic in which their partners are perversely dependent on them.

How can you tell if a man is trying to be important to you? Well, don't expect love poetry from most guys. Most of us find it to be of questionable utility.

Instead of words, look for deeds. Many good men show their love through what they view as caring behaviors, some of which are as unromantic as an oil change. Men and women frequently speak different languages, which is why so many couples have this stereotypical argument:

> *Her: "Sometimes I feel like you don't love me."*
> *Him: "How can you say that? If I didn't love you, I wouldn't be here."*
> *Her: "You never say it."*
> *Him (growing defensive): "I'm always doing things for you!"*

That sort of argument goes nowhere and leaves everyone feeling a little less loved. Before you can accurately judge a man's desire to be important to you, you have to know how he expresses affection. The best way to begin finding out is simply to ask. A good man will tell you.

Most men don't talk about it. We simply do what we think will win a place in your heart. We clean the gutters, repair a broken faucet, or make sure you never have to walk home alone. These actions are the love poetry of many kindhearted men.

A Good Man Maintains His Relationships

In my role as a psychologist, I generally don't care what couples argue about. They could argue over the winner of the 1952 World Series (it was the Yankees), how to handle money, or anything in between. I'm more concerned with *how* they argue. A kindhearted man isn't just kind when life is going smoothly. He's especially careful to be kind in the midst of conflict and disagreements.

Those are the moments he relies most heavily on the three pillars of a good man. His *purpose* is to maintain his relationship rather than let it fall apart. His *good mental health* gives him the foundation to disagree constructively. His *emotional maturity* gives him the coping skills and resourcefulness to treat you and the relationship with the importance you both deserve.

Arguing constructively, which includes understanding the other person's point of view, is a sign that he cares enough about the relationship to maintain it, even when he doesn't feel like doing so. He also maintains the relationship when it's going well and a lesser man might settle into complacency.

Curiosity may be one of the most reliable indicators that the relationship matters to him. The kindhearted man is interested in you and your life. His inquisitiveness will reveal itself, even if he avoids grueling relationship discussions that extend late into the night.

I've known many men who were hesitant to seek couple's therapy when their relationships were rocky, but their curiosity and drive to find more effective methods led them to my office. Their openness was key to repairing their relationships, and, without exception, the successful ones found some measure of joy in exploring ideas.

My grandfather, who was a farmer in his younger days, taught me to maintain tools. Clean them, oil them, and keep them out of the elements, he said. A bit of attentiveness will help them last indefinitely, and they won't let you down when you really need them. Good men maintain their relationships the way my grandfather maintained his plow. They understand the dangers of complacency.

Kindness can be challenging to assess, both because we sometimes lack healthy role models and because we quickly acclimate to unhealthy relationships. If there's any doubt you can trust your own perception on the matter of kindness, consider seeking the opinion of friends or family who may have a clearer view of his character.

The Cost of Overlooking Deficient Relationship Skills

Partnership with someone who has deficient relationship skills is a slow-motion train wreck. You'll be bored in calm waters after his charm has worn away; you'll be miserable when the storm hits and you have to do his share of the emotional work.

You've probably known a couple in which at least one partner is unskilled. These couples are usually caught in a cycle of exhausting drama. They really only communicate about their desires, goals, and relationship dynamics when they're deep in conflict. That's the worst time to for serious discussion, and so their conversations go poorly.

These couples are the romantic equivalent of the Three Stooges. At their best, they're woefully ineffective. At their worst, they're nasty and abusive. Partnering with a man who has deficient relationship skills ensures your eventual role in a depressing, emotional slapstick routine. That's precisely the type of problem you can avoid by selecting a man of solid emotional maturity.

One of the things that sometimes makes it difficult to recognize emotionally mature men is the fact that they're *not* spectacles to behold. Like a dependable car, they simply don't stand out. It's the broken-down wreck on the side of the road that gets all the attention—smoke billowing from its engine, and it's driver frantically trying to contain the situation. Meanwhile, the car that's firing on all cylinders quietly whizzes by.

Hopefully, I have painted a picture of what a man looks like when he is firing on all cylinders, emotionally. He's resilient, he's dependable when times are tough, he argues constructively, he's respected by others, and he's kind. Why accept anything less?

But we're not done yet. There is one more matter of import to discuss.

CHAPTER 10
SEEING HIM CLEARLY

Have your relationship mistakes seemed avoidable in retrospect? I know most of mine have. Maybe you've found yourself saying things like...

I should have listened to my friends.

I knew that person was going to be trouble.

I should have heeded my intuition.

That doesn't mean I regret all of my mistakes, and I don't think you should, either.

We all wear blinders of inexperience or self-deception. Where love is concerned, we can add the blinders born of infatuation and fantasy. It all leads to a wonderful treasure chest of successes and snafus we can use to inform future decisions. If you've made mistakes in love, then congratulations! You've earned wisdom.

Some people disregard their errors; others become immobilized by the shame. The sweet spot is somewhere between indifference and obsession, where we can make an honest appraisal of these valuable mistakes.

In this chapter, we're going to dissect ten conventional, well-intentioned thought processes that contribute to poor choices in men:

- ignoring red flags
- overlooking hidden treasures
- disregarding warnings from friends and family
- ignoring intuition
- excusing bad behavior
- drifting away from values
- insisting he function like a woman
- crusading to fix him
- clinging to sunk costs
- denying the common denominator

"Sunk cost" is a term borrowed from the business world. We'll discuss it below. "Common denominator" is borrowed from my fourth grade schoolteacher, Mrs. Unruh. I'll cover that one, too, but differently than she meant it. We will also look at two costly mistakes that leave women with entirely unsuitable partners: chasing the unavailable man and pursuing the personality-disordered man.

Ten Self-Deceptions That Create Poor Choices

If you could go back in time you'd probably have some wise words for your younger self about relationships. You might advise yourself to make different decisions about the men you have known. Now imagine you could go *forward* twenty years and talk to your current self and guide your decisions.

We can do that indirectly by listening to those with more experience. Learning from others is one of the qualities that separates us from fish. That, and gills. When a fish sees his buddy get yanked out of the water after he eats a plump worm, he doesn't think to himself, *Well I had a notion that worm was too promising to be true. I shall miss my friend Henry. I shall also learn from his mistake and avoid worms dangling suspiciously in the water.*

Nope. If you dangle the same hook in front of that fish's face, his actions will be ruled by instinct rather than intellect.

We're smarter than fish. Most of the time. There are moments when our instinct overpowers our intellect because we get caught up in some variety of wishful or erroneous thinking. The ten mistakes below are the errors of many people who have come before you.

This collection, to which others have so generously contributed, isn't about picking the right man. It is about seeing people *clearly.* Good men come into focus for any woman who avoids these common perceptual errors.

1. IGNORING RED FLAGS

This error is first on the list because it might be the most common. You're in plentiful company if you've ever made the mistake of ignoring warning signs.

Anne Boleyn was an educated and intelligent woman who married Henry VIII despite his cruel and unceremonious banishment of his first wife, Catherine. Years later, Henry took another mistress, just as he had taken Anne as a mistress while married to Catherine. Anne had ignored clear warning signs of the king's adulterous streak, and she paid with her head. The lesson is never date Henry VIII or anyone like him.

Neville Chamberlain, England's prime minister at the beginning of World War II, offers another grim example of ignoring red flags in his dealings with Adolf Hitler. By the time he began negotiations with Chamberlain, Hitler had a history of lying, but he sweet-talked Chamberlain into trusting him and—*surprise!*—he lied again.

It's human nature to ignore warning signs. Ironically, the heart and mind usually commit this error out of optimism. We hope for the best in others.

People also ignore warning signs when they fear there are no alternatives and so they settle for a substandard arrangement. (Desperation should be treated as an illusion. We usually have more options than we think.)

In other cases, especially for women, the motivation for ignoring red flags is one of politeness. We sometimes remain in a dangerous situation against our better judgment in order to avoid hurting someone's feelings. Make no mistake, predators can detect this vulnerability and shamelessly capitalize on it. Some are masters at persuading people to ignore their intuition.

There are plenty of reasons for staying involved when our higher selves know we should walk away. I encourage you to look back over your history to see if you have made this common error. If so, take an honest appraisal of your motivations for ignoring red flags. Were you driven by politeness? Desperation? Pressure? Did you fool yourself into believing a situation was better than it really was? Or that the alternatives were worse than they really were?

These are important questions. Be honest, and be compassionate with yourself. If you have a history of ignoring red flags, then this would be another excellent opportunity to write in a journal or even consult with a therapist to uncover your past motivations. We're less likely to repeat mistakes when we can clearly articulate their causes.

2. Overlooking Hidden Treasures

The guys who make the best relationship material—the *real* men possessing the three pillars—aren't always the first guys to catch a woman's attention.

Outstanding men sometimes make a poor first impression. Or they appear to be so bland that they make *no* first impression. They don't wear the right clothes, they're tongue-tied rather than confident, and they keep their best qualities safely hidden. By the time they are ready to show their true colors, the women they're interested in have moved on.

For some desirable, relationship-ready guys, this turns into a painful cycle in which they feel repeatedly rejected by women. That increases their jitters around women, which further reduces the likelihood of pursuing women and presenting themselves as the great catches they are.

Smart women see past the barriers these shy men build around themselves, and they understand the three pillars of a good man don't necessarily include irresistible charisma at first sight.

In the service of spotting hidden treasures in the future, you might devote some time to exploring your past. Do you have a history of regretting missed opportunities? If so, what desires, pressures, or training might have contributed to your decisions? And in retrospect, what were the qualities you admired in those men who got away?

3. DISREGARDING WARNINGS FROM FAMILY AND FRIENDS

Our eyes and ears point outward, not inward. That handy bit of biology keeps us from walking into coffee tables and open manholes. It also interferes with our self-perception. We don't clearly hear what we say or see what we do. We more clearly see how *others* behave.

We want to believe we possess acute insight, despite the obstructed view of our own behavior, and so it's easy to disregard warnings from friends and family when they're trying to say something we don't want to hear.

In addition to the natural impediments to our insight, humans can devise no end of rationalizations for running toward that metaphorical open manhole, especially where love is concerned. Maybe we're trying to prove love can conquer all. (It can't.) Maybe we believe an unhealthy relationship is the best we can do. (It isn't.) Maybe we simply aren't willing to stop fantasizing that this relationship will solve our problems. (It won't.)

To obscure warning signs even further, friends and family are sometimes subtle about their concerns. They might drop hints rather than risk hurting your feelings: "Are you sure you can trust him?" "Is he always so brash?" "He seems to have an unusual way of approaching people." Ignoring them is as easy as changing the subject.

Don't fall into that manhole. Listen to the warnings. Don't change the subject or defend him. Instead, get curious about what your friend or family member is seeing in him. If you hear a vaguely stated concern from a friend or loved one—like "I'm not so sure about him"—don't simply brush it aside. Ask what he or she means. If you hear something more specific—like "He sure drinks a lot—get curious about what your friend or loved one sees in his behavior.

Ask questions, assume they have your best interests at heart, and don't argue. You don't have to heed their warnings. Plenty of wonderful relationships begin without the blessings of friends and family. Just please hear them out.

There's one telltale sign when people are ignoring valuable warnings. They defend the relationship with statements like "He's not like that" or "This guy is different." If you hear yourself making such rationalizations, slow down and take a good look at the situation.

4. Ignoring Intuition

Useful omens don't always come in the form of red flags or warnings from friends. Sometimes the warning shows up in the form of an uncomfortable feeling. Ignoring intuition can be a big mistake, but infatuation can tempt us to disregard the wise little voice from within.

According to one study, gut feelings about a relationship can predict its later success. McNulty and colleagues (2013) noticed that newlyweds' implicit, automatic attitudes about their relationships more strongly predicted later satisfaction than their conscious, stated predictions. In other words, their gut feelings were more accurate than their thoughts.

Intuition is an awareness existing beneath conscious, verbal thought. It is a brilliant system. The mind picks up subtle signals that elude conscious perception and it warns us about dark clouds on the horizon. Unfortunately, it doesn't speak in words, and so it requires a willingness to heed easily ignored feelings and sensations.

If a gut feeling tells you something is amiss with the relationship, I ask you to take one simple action: stop. Slow down, and ask yourself what your intuition is trying to say.

5. EXCUSING BAD BEHAVIOR

Allow me to paint a scenario. You are at a party with your best friend and her new boyfriend. They begin to argue about something trivial. Maybe it's about last year's hockey championship, or who starred in the movie everyone saw in high school. He raises his voice and mocks her before storming off with his buddies to another part of the house and getting drunk.

He has treated her poorly, and he has done so publicly. You raise your concern about his behavior. "Does he always treat you so rudely?" you ask. She shrugs off your concern and says, "He's just under a lot of pressure these days."

It is natural to give our loved ones the benefit of a doubt. It's usually healthier than assuming the worst. But optimism is different from excusing boorish behavior. In this scenario, "pressure" is not the issue. Good men don't mistreat their partners when they're under stress.

Here's the difference between optimism and excuse-making. Optimism in this case refers to *your* perception of his behavior when his behavior is open to interpretation. For example, suppose during this scenario the man had tried to end the argument by saying, "you're adorable!" A defensive, pessimistic interpretation would color his words with dismissive condescension. You might think, *He's talking down to me! He thinks I'm too stupid to have a meaningful opinion!*

An optimistic interpretation, on the other hand, would assume he was trying to end the argument on a high note, even if the effort fell flat.

Making excuses is entirely different. It's an attempt to override the obvious effects of *his* behavior. In this scenario, he insulted your friend, embarrassed her, and abandoned her to get drunk. Any reasonable person would charge him with three counts of rudeness and wonder if his behavior reflects weakness of character. Excuse making is an attempt to protect him from deserved judgment. It is an act of self-deception. It rewards his bad behavior, and it encourages more of the same.

6. DRIFTING AWAY FROM VALUES

A relationship-ready man doesn't necessarily participate in everything you hold to be meaningful, but he is at least supportive and admiring of your values. One of the distinguishing features of terrible relationships is the attempt to separate one's partner from cherished activities and relationships.

It's just as damaging for people to voluntarily relinquish their values because they are smitten, or because they fear losing the relationship. Healthy relationships don't require you to abandon activities and relationships that matter to you.

7. EXPECTING MEN TO FUNCTION LIKE WOMEN

Remember the retreat-pursuit pattern we discussed in chapter 6? That's where one partner is anxiously trying to avoid an argument, while the other is anxiously trying to engage in an argument. Men and women are prone to certain misunderstandings thanks to the differences in the ways we process emotion. The retreat-pursuit pattern, and other gender-based hitches, are inflamed by women who expect men to function like women, and by men with the reverse expectation.

Intolerance for masculine and feminine traits creates conflict in relationships, plain and simple. The healthiest relationships value each. Yet, for many years, there has been a small but vocal anti-male contingent in Western society.

It begins in childhood, when school administrators replace tug-o-war with "tug-o-peace" and forbid dodgeball outright. It matters not that boys cherish these games, and that they gain important character traits from them. Even musical chairs and red rover have been attacked by misguided bureaucrats.

Rough-and-tumble games that boys crave—that they *need* for proper development—are condemned in favor of nurturing, noncompetitive activities (Hoff Sommers, 2013). The message to boys is clear: your boisterous, ambitious, male nature is unacceptable—and a little scary to bureaucratic types who feel bedeviled over the occasional skinned knee or bruised feelings.

The message carries forward into adulthood, when TV and movies routinely portray men as relationship buffoons while women are portrayed as nicer, wiser, and more caring. Careful research, however, has shown that men and women are equally altruistic, but in different ways. While women are likelier to be empathetic and nurturing, men are more likely to perform acts of kindness and assistance (Eagly 2009)—yet another example of how wonderfully complementary men and women are!

Even in my own profession, researchers and clinicians typically assume the "female" way of conducting relationships to be the correct way. I've heard countless colleagues advise men to suppress their natural tendencies. Men are told, for example, that protectiveness is controlling; that stoicism is cold; that the desire to quickly kiss and make up is avoidant and inauthentic.

These misunderstandings come at a price. Relationships go poorly for both men and women who believe the other gender is inherently flawed. Men who fail to recognize the value in feminine traits make cynical mate choices that turn out badly. Or they remain unhappy bachelors, simultaneously idealizing and denigrating the beauty of the feminine sensibility.

On the other side of this unnecessary divide, women who believe the myth that men handle emotion incorrectly risk prematurely rejecting terrific guys who might make ideal partners. And when they do find a partner, they assume themselves to be the emotional parent to a childlike galoot. That assumption leads to resentment on both sides.

The happiest couples I've known don't merely make room for the masculine and the feminine, they actually celebrate the differences. Really, is there any reason *not* to celebrate the person with whom you have decided to spend a lifetime?

8. CRUSADING TO FIX HIM

Life is distressingly short. It certainly is too short to spend our precious time trying to turn the wrong partner into the right one. Yet I'm sure we have all known people who have fallen in love with someone's potential and wasted years pointlessly trying to mold that person into someone new.

Men probably fall into the trap of "rescuing" mates as often as women, though in my clinical experience, men and women rescue and "fix" each other differently. Men who are compelled to be white knights tend to seek out women who have been mistreated and who they can "heal." Such misplaced chivalry is well-intentioned, but presumptuous.

Women who rescue men, if I may speak in further generalities, tend to seek out men who are projects. They seek men who have wonderful potential to be devoted, successful men but aren't quite there yet. They just need the love and guidance of a wise woman, or so the reasoning goes.

Don't kid yourself. A good, relationship-ready man doesn't need to be guided or cajoled into becoming a better man. He's already quietly working on it. He possesses the wisdom to know he's a work in progress and he is driven to improve.

Healthy couples help each other grow, but there's a difference between mutual growth and dragging him against his will. If you find yourself more concerned about his growth and progress than he is, then the relationship might be on shaky ground. That's a recipe for a boring romance because your personal growth will eventually leave him in the dust, and the gulf between you will widen. Plus, as the more mature one you'll be responsible for fixing every little problem he's unwilling to face. You'll resent him for his inertia, and he will resent you for your efforts to change him.

Sometimes his efforts aren't the problem. Sometimes both people are great partners, but their values are simply mismatched. Reconfiguring his priorities is not the answer. If you have a history of taking on "projects," I encourage you to explore your motivation for doing so. (Skilled psychologists get to the bottom of these questions quickly, saving people years of wasted effort.) Trying to change other people is sometimes a mask for an unanswered question within ourselves.

Wasting time on a "project" man can keep you hidden from the good man who's searching for you.

9. CLINGING TO SUNK COSTS

There is a phrase from the business world that applies to the dating scene. In business, a *sunk cost* is an unrecoverable expense. For example, past rent paid on a store front is gone forever, and so it should not influence current decisions.

In that example, it would be foolish to reinstate a costly and ineffective lease out of mere sentimentality, but our sense of allegiance to the property can lead us precisely to the wrong decision. Sometimes it makes more sense to find a property rather than doubling down on a past investment. Allowing irretrievable expenditures to influence current decisions can perpetuate costly mistakes—whether it's in business or in relationships.

Business people have to drill that idea into their minds because it is unnatural and counterintuitive. By our nature, humans don't like to lose material or waste effort. When we notice an investment of time, money, or love that hasn't paid off, we're prone to investing even more in order to avoid feeling that we have squandered resources. That's like thinking, *I overate yesterday, so I might as well overeat today*. Yesterday is gone. Today is a new day with new opportunities and new decisions.

A failing relationship is like a failing business. Yesterday's investment of love—all those months or years of trying to make it work—simply don't matter if a relationship is on life support and fading. The only real loss is the loss of priceless lessons and new opportunities forfeited while clinging to sunk costs.

10. DENYING THE COMMON DENOMINATOR

Have you ever met someone who seems to experience the same relationship problems over and over? They claim *every* landlord has been an unreasonable jerk, or *every* boss has been too demanding, or *every* boyfriend has been an uncaring clod.

Their repetitiveness comes from another little quirk of human nature: our difficulty recognizing when *we* are the common denominator.

The truth is, the person who bellyaches about a string of demanding bosses is probably lazy. The person who whines about every landlord probably has difficulty managing business relationships.

And the person who complains that every one of his or her former partners has behaved in the same fashion is probably making two mistakes: repeatedly choosing the same type of partner, and reenacting the same old counterproductive patterns.

If you find yourself complaining that every man you have dated has failed you in some similar way, then it might be time to explore an uncomfortable question: what are *you* doing to recreate painful experiences?

TWO TYPES OF MEN TO AVOID

Those ten little mistakes are tricky. They sneak up on a person, and they open the door to the wrong kind of relationships while shutting out the most desirable men. Mistakes that start small can be costly in the long run.

These next two relationship errors are serious. Like many of those we just discussed, they are often born of optimism, but they can cost the best years of your romantic life:

- pursuing the unavailable man
- courting the untreated, personality-disordered man

Unavailable and personality disordered men are the least capable of conducting long-term relationships. Unfortunately, they can be seductive and charismatic. Like an alluring, poisonous plant, avoid these men.

Pursuing the Unavailable Man

Sometimes reality is a real downer, like when the perfect mate is unavailable. It's even worse when an unavailable man lets you believe there's a chance for a relationship when there isn't. He relies on promises of future bliss, while in the present he avoids commitment—that is, until he wants something like attention, sex, or food. Every day with this man is a bouquet of lovely words negated by his unwillingness or inability to be a fully functioning romantic partner.

Not all unavailable men are manipulative Lotharios. Sometimes women waste their time pursuing nice guys who are…

Enthusiastic but otherwise occupied. He wants to be in a relationship, but all of his attention goes to work, hobbies, substances, or an existing romantic relationship from which he just can't tear himself away.

Willing but emotionally immature. Some men simply lack the skill for intimate relationships. They may not realize that relationships require more than declarations of intent.

Not in the market for love. One bit of unfortunate fallout from the gender wars of recent decades is the increasing number of men who are avoiding higher education, marriage, and fatherhood (H. Smith 2013). They feel hopeless about their prospects in love and work, and so they choose not to participate. This is a sad trend because it leaves fewer good men available than there would otherwise be. Take a man at his word when he says he is unwilling to commit.

Whatever the unavailable man's motivations, there are some warning signs that may indicate he lacks the ability or intent to truly commit to you. Unless you're satisfied being friends with benefits, watch for these troubling behaviors:

Excuses: The man who repeatedly says "I'll be able to commit as soon as I get a promotion/buy a house/finish softball season" is giving his relationship a low priority. Sometimes men stall for genuine and legitimate reasons. But he's telegraphing his unwillingness to commit if he wastes months and years of your time with excuses.

Physical absence: You deserve more than a string of text messages from a partner. The right man will desire time with you. Beware the man who only communicates electronically or otherwise avoids your physical presence. The relationship-ready man behaves like a friend. He wants to be around you.

Secretiveness: The man who shares little about himself and refuses to include you in his social or family circle is saying, "You're not really part of my life."

Self-centeredness: The man who knows little about you because the relationship centers almost entirely on him isn't really connecting with you. Too much of that behavior is the same as unavailability.

Disingenuousness: Unscrupulous men string gullible women along with double-talk and endless promises. If he fails to keep his words of devotion, then he's telling you something about his reliability and availability. Don't ignore the warning sign.

Post-intimacy desertion: Good men don't disappear after sex. If he is devoted to you, then his intention will most certainly extend to the hours and days after physical intimacy. The man who vanishes until the next romp might as well be scrawling it on the bathroom mirror: *I'm using you.*

A good, relationship-ready man leaves you feeling treasured, not used or abandoned. Don't make an unavailable man your white whale. Persistence is great; just don't dodge the facts. You might even enlist your friends and family to help you know when enough is enough. Life is too short to chase ghosts.

COURTING THE UNTREATED PERSONALITY-DISORDERED MAN

The term *personality disorder* refers to a group of mental health diagnoses that apply to people who have trouble navigating emotions and interpersonal relationships. Personality disorders involve a pattern of ineffective problem solving, unhealthy perceptions of self and others, and chaotic emotions. They involve relationships marred by conflict and chaos (American Psychiatric Association 2013). Here are some of the more notorious personality disorders:

Antisocial personality disorder: marked by a pattern of disregard for the rights of others. This person is charming, deceitful, manipulative, and destructive. The true sociopath views others as pawns to be used for his or her benefit.

Narcissistic personality disorder: grandiose, cold-hearted, and ruled by an overwhelming need to be the center of attention. There is no room for the needs of others when this person is in the room.

Borderline personality disorder: a pattern of broken relationships, unstable self-image, and emotional impulsivity. Relationships are consumed by emotional volatility and unpredictability. People with this personality style are unskilled at managing normal relationship friction, and they leave their partners fearing that any small incident could explode into a histrionic crisis.

Avoidant personality disorder: extreme social inhibition, persistent and irrational feelings of inadequacy, and hypersensitivity to negative evaluation. Relationships are constrained by this person's avoidance of social situations and their persistent fear of being criticized and rejected.

Dependent personality disorder: a pattern of submissive and clinging behavior resulting from an excessive need to be cared for. Relationships are overrun by the constant need for reassurance and assistance with even minor decisions.

That's just a partial list of disorders from the American Psychiatric Association. Rather than covering them all, it is more useful to understand the basic characteristics of disordered personality styles:

Emotional experience is intense and inflexible. They experience disproportionate or unbefitting emotional reactions, and they have yet to develop a range of nuanced emotional skills. They instead rely on a handful of brute-force techniques such as tantrums, manipulation, or avoidance. They struggle to manage emotional impulse.

Thoughts about self and others lack complexity. They tend to view themselves and others as all-good or all-bad, rather than viewing people as complex individuals possessing diverse characteristics. Their behavior is driven by this lack of emotional complexity.

In other words, if you're in a relationship with a personality-disordered man, his treatment of you may be governed by his momentary feelings rather than his principles. Life is great when he's happy; life is miserable when he's sad, mad, or feeling victimized. Some personality disorders lead people to view others merely as potential victims or potential abusers. It's no fun to be cast in either role.

Relationship behavior is ineffective. Their attempts to manage conflict are driven by insecurity and emotional chaos. They struggle to tolerate discomfort, and their conflict-management style is counterproductive. They have interpersonal problems with bosses, family members, and friends, adding further burden to intimate partners who must serve as a constant source of comfort.

Does this mean you should *never* date someone with a personality disorder? Absolutely not. Like people who have fought their way through emotional difficulties or substance abuse, people with maladaptive personality styles can develop exceptional insight and abilities, provided they are willing to do the work. Successful treatment requires a great deal of effort and long-term commitment, during which they need to establish support outside their romantic relationship so they do not overburden their partners.

Some disorders are notoriously resistant to treatment, particularly antisocial personality disorder, which has a lifetime prevalence of about 5 percent among men (Oltmanns and Powers 2012). Being antisocial can be fun and profitable, which is why these people are rarely motivated to change. Narcissistic personality disorder is also famously impenetrable because, by definition, narcissistic people don't recognize their own shortcomings.

Personality disorders are not particularly rare. One careful study estimated that approximately 7 percent of middle-aged adults fit into at least one category (Oltmanns et al. 2014). Other estimates run as high as 9.1 percent of the adult population (Lenzenweger et al. 2007).

Though precise numbers are hard to pin down, anyone searching for a mate should be aware of these disorders. Some of them involve traits that are quite alluring at first. People with antisocial, narcissistic, or borderline personality styles can be unusually charming and charismatic.

Even the disorders that are not characterized by charm, such as dependent or avoidant personality disorders, may be especially attractive to people who have a desire to be needed.

Life with people suffering from an untreated personality disorder can be chaotic and miserable. It can leave partners feeling as if they're always walking on eggshells, and that everything they do is bound to cause a histrionic fight. These poor partners end up carrying the burden of the relationship, apologizing on their partner's behalf, and suffering the brain-deadening effects of the metaphorical emotional poverty we discussed in chapter 6.

Personality disorders are no fun for the sufferer, either. They are often in tremendous emotional pain. Borderline personality disorder appears to be particularly destructive to marriages, leading to both low general satisfaction and high levels of verbal aggression (Oltmanns and Powers 2012).

It can take years of chaos before the uninitiated realize a partner suffers with one of these conditions, especially for anyone prone to the ten vision-clouding mistakes we discussed earlier in the chapter.

This may seem like an uncomfortable and unforgiving idea, but people suffering from personality disorders must learn different and more effective ways of thinking, acting, and managing emotion in order to succeed in close relationships. You might consider a more emotionally stable relationship if you're not up for the challenge of supporting someone through such an arduous journey.

Clarity of vision means seeing a man's emotional skills and availability for what they really are, and acknowledging one's own tendency to distort reality. My hope for this chapter is to help you recognize Mr. Right when he glides (or stumbles) into your field of vision.

CHAPTER 11
WHERE IS MR. RIGHT?

We've covered a wide variety of men, some shiny and some tarnished. Now let's discuss the most important man in this book: Mr. Right. No matter what his particulars might be, he possesses the three pillars of a good man:

- sense of purpose
- good mental health
- emotional maturity

Perhaps this book has convinced you that you have already found Mr. Right. If so, I couldn't be happier! But please keep reading because there are some things to know about living with a good man.

If you are still searching for Mr. Right, you might be wondering where to meet him. I wish this book had the power to make him materialize, but it doesn't. Nor will his car conveniently break down in front of your house on a random Tuesday evening. It's up to you to create the opportunity to cross paths with him, but luckily the formula is simple. It is really just a game of numbers. The more people you know, and the more open you are about your intention to find a wonderful relationship, the likelier you are to encounter him.

Good men are everywhere. He might have a terrible marketing department, but Mr. Right is searching for you, and he's hoping you will notice him. I hope you have faith in his existence because we usually find what we're looking for.

That's not new-age psychobabble. We see the world through a lens of expectations that obscures our ability to recognize people and possibilities outside that restricted view. If history or training has taught you to expect men to treat you poorly, then your mind will see poorly behaving men everywhere. The mind is capable of overlooking decent men as if they don't exist. Expectations are powerful shapers of perception.

Expectation is why the wealthy tend to remain wealthy: they are comfortable with money, they expect to have it, and so they naturally perceive paths to wealth. Expectation is why the likelihood of divorce increases with each failed marriage: each successive dissolution makes divorce seem more normal. And expectation is why boys whose fathers abandoned them are slightly more prone to abandon their own children: their view of fatherhood is constrained by the warped lens they inherited.

We humans are awfully predictable. We do what we know how to do, and we find what we expect to find—that is, until we discover a new way of viewing and approaching the world. We may not control what our minds anticipate, but we can choose to disregard its expectations.

There's even more good news. We have an endless capacity to alter and expand our expectations. That's how the poor become wealthy; it's how divorced people build lasting marriages; it's how fatherless boys grow into outstanding and devoted fathers. We can change our destiny by altering our expectations. That includes our expectations about love and the opposite sex.

This book does not hold men to unrealistic expectations. Not at all. Virtuous men want to be judged by high expectations because otherwise they lose faith in the judgment of women, and they lose hope for love. But when you expect men to possess purpose, good mental health, and emotional maturity, then Mr. Right knows he has a chance at winning your heart.

WHAT MR. RIGHT IS LOOKING FOR

Men of purpose, good mental health, and emotional maturity also possess high standards for the women they allow into their lives. They want a partner with similar values, great communication skills, emotional maturity, strength of character, and a bright and curious mind.

While writing *The Woman's Guide to How Men Think*, I surveyed hundreds of men to discover what they're looking for in relationships. If I were to distill their thoughts to one idea, it would be that good men are looking for women who know how to be happy in romance.

We men are generally uncomplicated and fairly binary in our emotional states. We're either fearful or secure, confused or certain, chatty or quiet, hungry or full. More often than not, a good man is content.

We men take happiness seriously. Maybe that's because we don't live as long as women, or maybe it's because our shoes don't mangle our feet. Whatever the reason, good men are usually happy. Why else would they have invented fishing poles that fit right in your pocket, or attached bottle openers to everything from belt buckles to cell phones? You never know when the opportunity for fun will present itself!

Men want life to improve as the years pass, and the data says we become happier with age. Men peak in happiness around the age of sixty, and men are generally the happier gender throughout most of the lifespan (Sutin et al. 2013).

Why does male happiness increase with age? The twenties and thirties are arguably the most stressful times in a man's life. He faces questions of career, and traditionally he has been confronted with the challenge of supporting others. Men across cultures are expected to make themselves useful or suffer harsh judgment. The question of their usefulness is best settled early in life.

Few men are unhappy while confronting those challenges. We're mostly content, even during the tough years, because good men appreciate challenges. But we also get happier as those challenges recede, and life gets easier.

We could easily become jaded and miserable, beaten down by the demands of life and the ravages of time. Some men do, but most men choose the brighter path of enjoying the moment. We're looking for women who can do the same.

Men are happy when life is smooth, and so we spend a lot of time and effort trying to improve ourselves and eliminate problems. The Internet has scads of websites, by men and for men, to help us become better men. We want to be better at grilling, fathering, dressing, and fixing. Those websites exist because most men crave improvement and joy.

We men have known for countless generations that personality is not fixed. Motivated people can grow and change. Over time and with effort, people can even alter fundamental personality traits.

For example, people can become more agreeable, more patient, more goal oriented, and more open to experience. These changes can endure, and they can improve quality of life more than other types of life changes, like becoming wealthy (Boyce, Wood, and Powdthavee 2013).

Those who believe personality and intelligence are malleable can change their personalities; those who believe these qualities are fixed are likely to remain the same (Dweck 2008). Good men reflect on what it means to be a man, and they adjust their personalities accordingly. I think the desire to improve begins with our boyhood training that says, *Don't hurt people. Be valuable.*

Men of virtue and service also know that part of being valuable is possessing a positive disposition. It is simply more fun to be around a happy person.

Good men desire women who are willing and able to join them on the road to happiness. We want our relationships to be simple and fun. We want to eliminate conflict quickly and get on with the business of living happy lives with the women of our dreams.

In addition to happiness, there are a few other items only the right woman can provide. Let's take a look at those now.

WHAT ONLY YOU CAN GIVE HIM

The world doesn't make it easy for a man to have a meaningful and relevant existence. His boss doesn't appreciate him. His customers don't care about him. The tax man is only interested in a hefty slice of his paycheck. He's useful only as long as he dresses the part, acts the role, and provides the goods. Ultimately, he is expendable, and he knows it. Another man can always take his place in the world.

Home is the exception. Home is his haven. It is the one place he can feel truly loved, accepted, and appreciated. A good man feels great when his partner understands his masculine qualities, but he's on top of the world when she truly appreciates him.

He feels valuable when he knows how to please you. Believe it or not, there are women (and men) who are impossible to please. That's misery for a man who lives to serve, so make sure he knows he can please you, and make sure he knows how. He can't read your mind, so you may need to tell him your path to happiness. Please don't torture him by saying, "You would know what I want if you loved me."

One stereotypical male quality women sometimes find vexing is the ability to "turn off" the relationship when he's engaged in other matters. Women, more than men, have a wonderful ability to feel connected to their partners even when they're separated by time and distance. Men lives tend to be more compartmentalized. When you ask, "Did you think of me today?" the honest answer is sometimes, "No." But that doesn't mean you aren't the center of his universe.

Men's ability to temporarily uncouple might come from the way in which men and women evolved together. Until fairly recently in human history, men would leave the village to slay large, dangerous animals in order to feed the clan. They probably couldn't afford to pine away for their loved ones back home. And truthfully, they were probably having fun. But when the hunt was over, I'm certain they wanted nothing more than the warmth of their families. I imagine they were never happier to see their women than when they returned home feeling like men.

Smart couples make room for their partners' traits, especially the most vexing qualities. A woman who appreciates her man's ability to compartmentalize his life also knows he will be joyful and present when he returns from slaying the metaphorical beast.

There are a few common mistakes women make that can leave men feeling unappreciated. If these mistakes go on long enough, even the most optimistic man will feel hopeless and give up on the relationship (S. T. Smith 2013):

> **Time traveling:** Men tend to compartmentalize arguments, preferring to solve problems that exist here and now, rather than addressing past events or future possibilities. Women generally have a more developed ability to attend to themes in relationships, and in my clinical experience, women are likelier to bring up past conflicts during the current one. This often leaves men feeling overwhelmed and defensive. I'm not suggesting a woman should suppress her concerns about the past or future. Couples should discuss anything that bothers either partner. Just bear in mind that most men are better able to handle one issue at a time.

Bearing grudges: Women have told me they are baffled by the male ability to forgive and forget. It's true. Men really are trained to shake hands and move on. This complicates intimate relationships, where risks are high. Lack of forgiveness from women is highly anxiety provoking for men.

It's no great threat if a stranger refuses to forgive a transgression, but it is unsettling when a loved one bears a grudge. It fuels doubt about the relationship. This is especially tough on men because we are driven to please, and it tortures us when a partner bears a grudge over small transgressions and misunderstandings.

Forgiveness sometimes involves sitting with the uncomfortable feeling that something is unresolved even when we know, logically, that it's time to move on. Luckily, that discomfort fades. Tolerating it can be far preferable to the long-term damage that comes from indulging it.

Punishing him for talking: Have you ever seen a dog owner scold a dog when it returns after venturing too far? "Bad dog! You come when I call you!" To the dog's mind, the lesson is *Don't come when you're called or you'll be punished.* Smart dog owners know when to praise their pets. Dogs should be rewarded for returning, even if the owner is feeling upset.

Some women make a similar error when their man finally opens up to them. They say things like "Why didn't you say something sooner?" or "How can you feel that way?" To a man's mind, the lesson is *I disappoint her when I talk, therefore I won't talk.* The wiser response is acceptance and understanding, even when the timing or the message isn't what you were hoping for.

Expecting him to read your mind: It's been said a thousand times, and my clinical experience says it's worth repeating: sometimes we men don't know what you want until you tell us. Your needs and desires may be obvious to you, and we really wish we could see them as clearly as you do, but sometimes we simply can't. There have even been movies in which a man's ability to read a woman's mind is portrayed as a superpower.

The wise woman focuses on her man's overriding desire to please her, not his momentary shortcomings. Focusing on the latter will only discourage him, and eventually he may stop trying altogether.

Avoiding solutions: Another age-old gender stereotype is the male-female tug-of-war over solutions versus empathy. The stereotypical female desire is to be heard and supported. The stereotypical man wants to skip the complex discussion and get right to the answer. Both end up feeling unsatisfied and unheard. The wise woman tells her partner when she simply wants to be heard. Remember, he can't read your mind. She also allows him to offer solutions at some point, even if it's only to get them off his chest. (Sometimes he needs to be heard, too.)

A happy, healthy relationship is the center of a good man's world. Sure, we venture out to work and play, but good men always want to come home, where we're accepted, loved, and appreciated. Don't believe it? Even that manliest of role models for men, General George S. Patton, corresponded religiously with his beloved Beatrice while he was beating up the Nazis. We know we are better men when we have earned the love of a good and kind woman.

So where is Mr. Right? He's looking for your love to complete his world, and he's hoping you will recognize him for the good man he is.

THE 12-POINT INVENTORY

This inventory is based on the principles in chapters 7 through 9. I hope you will peer into the future a bit as you explore these inventory items with a particular man in mind. Ask yourself, *Will his qualities appeal to you ten years hence? Will they be useful if you raise a family together? Will his personality still be sexy when you are both old and gray?*

Please also take his age and experience into account. You wouldn't expect a twenty-year-old to possess the wisdom and maturity of a man twice his age, but both men should crave personal growth. Good men always consider themselves works in progress.

I've intentionally provided no scoring system beyond this scale for each item:

Strongly Disagree | *Disagree* | *Uncertain* | *Agree* | *Strongly Agree*

Please feel free to rate or record your answers in any way you see fit, though I recommend giving due consideration to any items with a "Strongly Disagree" rating. They might be warning signs you shouldn't ignore. I'll leave it to your judgment how many answers of "Uncertain" or "Disagree" you might find tolerable in the distant future, though I'd caution you against overestimating when you and he are in the throes of infatuation.

You might find yourself equivocating if your responses to these items are unpleasant. You might think, *He's really not that bad* or *Maybe this question doesn't matter.*

Don't let your mind get away with trying to rescue him from a harsh evaluation. And don't let it protect you from a harsh reality. Take your time with each item. Journal about your responses, if you're so inclined, and don't let your heart alone run the show. Listen to your intuition, your values, your intellect, your friends and loved ones.

Finally, I encourage you to have fun and include him in the process. Share this inventory with him, and be prepared to respond to similar items in return. He should be just as curious about you as you are about him.

THE 12-POINT INVENTORY

1. His values are compatible with mine (chapter 7).

- We share similar definitions of excitement.
- He supports my goals, and I support his.
- Our values are similar enough that our differences are easy to tolerate.

Strongly Disagree | Disagree | Uncertain | Agree | Strongly Agree

My thoughts and feelings on this item:

_____

_____

_____

_____

_____

2. He is part of something larger than himself (chapter 7).

- He pursues a passion outside the relationship.
- His outside interests are consistent with values I can support.
- He is able to balance his individual pursuits and his relationships.

Strongly Disagree | Disagree | Uncertain | Agree | Strongly Agree

My thoughts and feelings on this item:

_____

_____

_____

_____

_____

3. He maintains his man card (chapter 7).

- He strives to contribute more to relationships than he takes from them.
- He surrounds himself with respectable men.
- He is thoughtful about the effect his actions have on others.

Strongly Disagree | Disagree | Uncertain | Agree | Strongly Agree

My thoughts and feelings on this item:

_____

_____

_____

_____

_____

4. He is striving to be honorable (chapter 7).

- He is respected by others because he keeps his word and meets his commitments.
- He behaves honorably even when he is under stress.
- He behaves honorably even in small matters.

Strongly Disagree | Disagree | Uncertain | Agree | Strongly Agree

My thoughts and feelings on this item:

_____

_____

_____

_____

_____

5. He does not rely on substances or other forms of avoidance (chapter 8).

- People around him do not hint or joke that he is an alcoholic or an addict.
- I do not find myself rationalizing or covering for his substance use or other forms of avoidance.
- His escapes are healthy, temporary, and rejuvenating.

Strongly Disagree | Disagree | Uncertain | Agree | Strongly Agree

My thoughts and feelings on this item:

_____

_____

_____

_____

_____

6. He handles manly stoicism well (chapter 8).

- He is able to express and discuss emotions other than anger and happiness.
- He is able to verbalize his thoughts when he is angry, ashamed, disappointed, or sad.
- He is interested in my emotional experience and the emotional experiences of others.

Strongly Disagree | Disagree | Uncertain | Agree | Strongly Agree

My thoughts and feelings on this item:

_____

_____

_____

_____

_____

7. He values insight (chapter 8).

- He does not routinely turn "weak" emotions like sadness into "strong" emotions like anger or jealousy.
- He is able to identify how his history affects his current thoughts, feelings, and behaviors.
- He identifies and takes responsibility for his part in conflicts.

Strongly Disagree | Disagree | Uncertain | Agree | Strongly Agree

My thoughts and feelings on this item:

_____

_____

_____

_____

_____

8. He is available (chapter 8).

- His relationship history reflects a desire to commit.
- His words about commitment fit with his behavior toward me.
- I do not find myself ignoring signs that he is less committed to the relationship than I am.

Strongly Disagree | Disagree | Uncertain | Agree | Strongly Agree

My thoughts and feelings on this item:

_____

_____

_____

_____

_____

9. He handles bad moods and bad days well (chapter 9).

- He takes care of his body and mind.
- He has a positive and reliable support system.
- He does not withdraw from problems; he solves them.

Strongly Disagree | Disagree | Uncertain | Agree | Strongly Agree

My thoughts and feelings on this item:

_____

_____

_____

_____

_____

10. He handles adversity well (chapter 9).

- He has grown in identifiable ways from difficulties in his life.
- He is able to create and follow a plan to conquer challenges.
- I would want him on my team if I needed help.

Strongly Disagree | Disagree | Uncertain | Agree | Strongly Agree

My thoughts and feelings on this item:

_____

_____

_____

_____

_____

11. He is kind to others (chapter 9).

- He speaks respectfully of his family, friends, and past romantic partners, even when he disagrees with them.
- He treats people well, even when he doesn't have to.
- He gets his needs met in a straightforward and honest manner.

Strongly Disagree | Disagree | Uncertain | Agree | Strongly Agree

My thoughts and feelings on this item:

_____

_____

_____

_____

_____

12. He is kind to me (chapter 9).

- I would want my best friend to be treated the way he treats me.
- He demonstrates a desire to be important to me.
- I feel relaxed and comfortable in his presence.

Strongly Disagree | Disagree | Uncertain | Agree | Strongly Agree

My thoughts and feelings on this item:

_____

_____

_____

_____

_____

References

Allgood, S. M., T. E. Beckert, and C. Peterson. 2012. "The Role of Father Involvement in the Perceived Psychological Well-Being of Young Adult Daughters: A Retrospective Study." *North American Journal of Psychology* 14:95–110.

American Psychiatric Association. 2013. *Diagnostic and Statistical Manual of Mental
Disorders.* 5th edition. Washington, DC: Author.

Archuleta, K.L. 2011. "Couples, Money, and Expectations: Negotiating Financial Management Roles to Increase Relationship Satisfaction." *Marriage &
Family Review* 49:391–411.

Atlantis, E., K. Lange, R. D. Goldney, S. Martin, M. T. Haren, A. Taylor, P. D.
O'Loughlin, V. Marshall, W. Tilley, and G. A. Wittert. 2011. "Specific Medical Conditions Associated with Clinically Significant Depressive Symptoms
in Men." *Social Psychology and Psychiatric Epidemiology* 46:1303–1312.

Baumeister, R. 2010. *Is There Anything Good About Men? How Cultures Flourish by
Exploiting Men.* New York: Oxford University Press.

Berghoff, C. R., A. M. Pomerantz, J. C. Pettibone, D. J. Segrist, and D. R. Bed-
well. 2012. "The Relationship Between Experiential Avoidance and Impulsiveness in a Nonclinical Sample." *Behaviour Change* 29:25–35.

Blonigen, D. M., T. Burroughs, J. R. Haber, and T. Jacob. 2013. "Psychiatric
Morbidity Is Linked to Problem Drinking in Midlife Among Alcohol-Depen-

dent Men: A Co-Twin Control Study." *Journal of Studies on Alcohol and Drugs* 74:136–140.

Bloomfield, M. A. P., C. J. A. Morgan, A. Egerton, S. Kapur, H. V. Curran, and O. D. Howes. 2014. "Dopaminergic Function in Cannabis Users and Its Relationship to Cannabis-Induced Psychotic Symptoms." *Biological Psychiatry* 75:470–478.

Boden, J. M., D. M. Fergusson, and L. J. Horwood. 2010. "Cigarette Smoking and Depression: Tests of Causal Linkages Using a Longitudinal Birth Cohort." *The British Journal of Psychiatry* 196:440–446.

Bodenmann, G., S. Pihet, and K. Kayser. 2006. "The Relationship Between Dyadic Coping and Marital Quality: A 2-Year Longitudinal Study." *Journal of Family Psychology* 20:485–493.

Bosson, J. K., and J. A. Vandello. 2011. "Precarious Manhood and Its Links to Action and Aggression." *Current Directions in Psychological Science* 20:82–86.

Boyce, C. J., A. M. Wood, and N. Powdthavee. 2013. "Is Personality Fixed? Personality Changes as Much as 'Variable' Economic Factors and More Strongly Predicts Changes to Life Satisfaction." *Social Indicators Research* 111:287–305.

Brunstein, J. C., O. C. Schultheiss, and R. Grässmann. 1998. "Goals and Emotional Well-Being: The Moderating Role of Motive Dispositions." *Journal of Personality and Social Psychology* 75:494–508.

Burns, A., and R. Dunlop. 2002. "Parental Marital Quality and Family Conflict: Longitudinal Effects on Adolescents from Divorcing and Non-Divorcing Families." *Journal of Divorce & Remarriage* 37:57–74.

Bushman, B. J. 2002. "Does Venting Anger Feed or Extinguish the Flame? Catharsis, Rumination, Distraction, Anger, and Aggressive Responding." *Personality & Social Psychology Bulletin* 28:724–731.

Buss, D. M., and M. Barnes. 1986. "Preferences in Human Mate Selection." *Journal of Personality and Social Psychology* 50:559–570.

Buss, D. M., and D. P. Schmidt. 1993. "Sexual Strategies Theory: An Evolutionary Perspective on Human Mating." *Psychological Review* 100:204–232.

Byrd-Craven, J., B. J. Auer, D. A. Granger, and A. R. Massey. 2012. "The Father–Daughter Dance: The Relationship Between Father–Daughter Relationship Quality and Daughters' Stress Response." *Journal of Family Psychology* 26:87–94.

Centers for Disease Control and Prevention. 2012. "Suicide: Facts at a Glance." Accessed November 12, 2013. http://www.cdc.gov/violenceprevention/pdf/suicide-datasheet-a.pdf.

Coleman, D., M. S. Kaplan, and J. T. Casey. 2011. "The Social Nature of Male Suicide: A New Analytic Model." *International Journal of Men's Health* 10:240–252.

Compton, W. M., Y. F. Thomas, F. S. Stinson, and B. F. Grant. 2007. "Prevalence, Correlates, Disability, and Comorbidity of DSM-IV Drug Abuse and Dependence in the United States: Results from the National Epidemiologic Survey on Alcohol and Related Conditions." *Archives of General Psychiatry* 64:566–576.

Costa, P. T., and R. R. McCrae. 1992. *The NEO PI-R Professional Manual*. Odessa, FL: Psychological Assessment Resources.

Dahl, J. C., J. C. Plumb, I. Stewart, and T. Lundgren. 2009. *The Art and Science of Valuing in Psychotherapy*. Oakland, CA: New Harbinger.

Davis, E., E. Greenberger, S. Charles, C. Chen, L. Zhao, and Q. Dong. 2012. "Emotion Experience and Regulation in China and the United States: How Do Culture and Gender Shape Emotion Responding?" *International Journal of Psychology* 47:230–239.

Del Russo, J. M. 2010. "Emotionally Absent Fathers and Their Adult Daughters' Relationships with Men." *Dissertation Abstracts International: Section B: The Sciences and Engineering* 70:5814.

Dufner, M., J. F. Rauthmann, A. Z. Czarna, and J. J. A. Denissen. 2013. "Are Narcissists Sexy? Zeroing in on the Effect of Narcissism on Short-Term-Mate Appeal." *Personality and Social Psychology Bulletin* 39:870–882.

Dweck, C. S. 2008. "Can Personality Be Changed? The Role of Beliefs in Personality and Change." *Current Directions in Psychological Science* 17:391–394.

Eagly, A. H. 2009. "The His and Hers of Prosocial Behavior: An Examination of the Social Psychology of Gender." *American Psychologist* 64:644–658.

Farbman, D. 2002. "The Sleeper Effect: Truth or Fiction. Comparing the Intimate Relationships of Single Daughters of Divorce and Single Daughters of Intact Families." *Dissertation Abstracts International: Section B: The Sciences and Engineering* 62:3797.

Gallagher, J. J. 2008. "The Father-Daughter Relationship: A Father's Impact on His Daughter's Psychological Development: With Particular Focus on a Daughter's Formation of Adult Intimate Relationships." *Dissertation Abstracts International: Section B: The Sciences and Engineering* 69:2624.

Garfield, C. F., A. Isacco, and W. D. Bartlo. 2010. "Men's Health and Fatherhood in the Urban Midwestern United States." *International Journal of Men's Health* 9:161–174.

Goetz, C. D. 2013. "What Do Women's Advertised Mate Preferences Reveal? An Analysis of Video Dating Profiles." *Evolutionary Psychology* 11:383–391.

Green, J. D., and M. E. Addis. 2012. "Individual Differences in Masculine Gender Socialization as Predictive of Men's Psychophysiological Responses to Negative Affect." *International Journal of Men's Health* 11:63–82.

Greenberg, S. T., S. J. Shepard, C. D. Chuick, and S. V. Cochran. 2009. "Clinical and Personality Features of Depressed College Males: An Exploratory Investigation." *International Journal of Men's Health* 8:169–177.

Hagemeyer, B., W. Neberich, J. B. Asendorpf, and F. J. Neyer. 2012. "(In)Congruence of Implicit and Explicit Communal Motives Predicts the Quality and Stability of Couple Relationships." *Journal of Personality* 81:390–402.

Hanna, E. Z., and Grant, B. F. 1997. "Gender Differences in DSM-IV Alcohol Use Disorders and Major Depression as Distributed in the General Population: Clinical Implications." *Comprehensive Psychiatry* 38:202–212.

Herzberg, P. Y. 2013. "Coping in Relationships: The Interplay Between Individual and Dyadic Coping and Their Effects on Relationship Satisfaction." *Anxiety, Stress, and Coping* 26:136–153.

Hirvonen, J., R. S. Goodwin, C. T. Li, G. E. Terry, S. S. Zoghbi, C. Morse, V. W. Pike, N. D. Volkow, M. A. Huestis, and R. B. Innis. 2011. "Reversible and Regionally Selective Downregulation of Brain Cannabinoid CB1 Receptors in Chronic Daily Cannabis Smokers." *Molecular Psychiatry* 6:642–649.

Hoff Sommers, C. 2013. *The War Against Boys: How Misguided Policies Are Harming Our Young Men.* New York: Simon & Schuster.

Holmila, M., and K. Raitasalo. 2005. "Gender Differences in Drinking: Why Do They Still Exist?" *Addiction* 100:1763–1769.

Huoviala, P., and M. J. Rantala. 2013. "A Putative Human Pheromone, Androstadienone, Increases Cooperation Between Men." *PLoS ONE* 8:e62499.

Job, V., K. Bernecker, and C. S. Dweck. 2012. "Are Implicit Motives the Need to Feel Certain Affect? Motive-Affect Congruence Predicts Relationship Satisfaction." *Personality and Social Psychology Bulletin* 38:1552–1565.

Jones, A. 2009. "The Impact of the Father-Daughter Dyad on Female Sexuality, Self-Concept, and Interpersonal Relationships with Men." *Dissertation Abstracts International: Section B: The Sciences and Engineering* 70:1368.

Judge, T. A., B. A. Livingston, and C. Hurst. 2012. "Do Nice Guys—and Gals—Really Finish Last? The Joint Effects of Sex and Agreeableness on Income." *Journal of Personality and Social Psychology* 102:390–407.

Karekla, M., and G. Panayiotou. 2011. "Coping and Experiential Avoidance: Unique or Overlapping Constructs?" *Journal of Behavior Therapy and Experimental Psychiatry* 42:163–170.

Keyes, K. M., S. S. Martins, C. Blanco, and D. S. Hasin. 2010. "Telescoping and Gender Differences in Alcohol Dependence: New Evidence from Two National Surveys." *The American Journal of Psychiatry* 167:969–976.

Kilmann, P. R., J. M. C. Vendemia, M. M. Parnell, and G. C. Urbaniak. 2009. "Parent Characteristics Linked with Daughters' Attachment Styles." *Adolescence* 44:557–568.

Kovess-Masfety, V., J. Alonso, M. Angermeyer, E. Bromet, G. de Girolamo, P. de Jonge, K. Demyttenaere, S. E. Florescu, M. J. Gruber, O. Gureje, C. Hu, Y.

Huang, E. G. Karam, R. Jin, J. Lépine, D. Levinson, K. A. McLaughlin, M. E. Medina-Mora, S. O'Neill, Y. Ono, J. A. Posada-Villa, N. A. Sampson, K. M. Scott, V. Shahly, D. J. Stein, M. C. Viana, Z. Zarkov, and R. C. Kessler. 2013. "Irritable Mood in Adult Major Depressive Disorder: Results From the World Mental Health Surveys." *Depression and Anxiety* 30:395–406.

Kreider, R. M., and R. Ellis. 2011. "Number, Timing, and Duration of Marriages and Divorces: 2009." *Current Population Reports*, P70-125, US Census Bureau, Washington, DC.

Lazarus, R. S. 1993. "Coping Theory and Research: Past, Present, and Future." *Psychosomatic Medicine* 55:234–247.

Lenzenweger, M. F., M. C. Lane, A. W. Loranger, and R. C. Kessler. 2007. "DSM-IV Personality Disorders in the National Comorbidity Survey Replication." *Biological Psychiatry* 62:553–564.

Lowenstein, L. F. 2005. "Causes and Associated Features of Divorce as Seen by Recent Research." *Journal of Divorce & Remarriage* 42:153–171.

Maier, W., M. Gänsicke, R. Gater, M. Rezaki, B. Tiemens, and R. Florenzano Urzúa. 1999. "Gender Differences in the Prevalence of Depression: A Survey in Primary Care." *Journal of Affective Disorders* 53:241–252.

Mani, A., S. Mullainathan, E. Shafir, and J. Zhao. 2013. "Poverty Impedes Cognitive Function." *Science* 341:976–980.

Mansfield, A. K., and J. V. Cordova. 2007. "A Behavioral Perspective on Adult Attachment Style, Intimacy, and Relationship Health." In *Understanding Behavioral Disorders: A Contemporary Behavioral Perspective*, edited by D. W. Woods and J. Kanter. Oakland, CA: Context Press.

Martin, L. A., H. W. Neighbors, and D. M. Griffith. 2013. "The Experience of Symptoms of Depression in Men vs. Women: Analysis of the National Comorbidity Survey Replication." *JAMA Psychiatry* 70:1100–1106.

Mckinley, D. 1997. "Shared Values Among Couples as a Prognosis for Marital Satisfaction." *Dissertation Abstracts International: Section B: The Sciences and Engineering* 58:2752.

McLean, C. P., and E. R. Anderson. 2009. "Brave Men and Timid Women? A Review of the Gender Differences in Fear and Anxiety." *Clinical Psychology Review* 29:496–505.

McNulty, J. K., M. A. Olson, A. L. Meltzer, and M. J. Shaffer. 2013. "Though They May Be Unaware, Newlyweds Implicitly Know Whether Their Marriage Will Be Satisfying." *Science* 342:1119–1120.

Meier, M. H., A. Caspi, A. Ambler, H. Harrington, R. Houts, R. S. E. Keefe, K. McDonald, A. Ward., R. Poulton., and T. E. Moffitt. 2012. "Persistent Cannabis Users Show Neuropsychological Decline from Childhood to Midlife." *PNAS Proceedings of the National Academy of Sciences of the United States of America* 109:E2657–E2664.

Merikangas, K. R., J. He, M. Burstein, S. A. Swanson, S. Avenevoli, L. Cui, C. Benjet, K. Georgiades, and J. Swendsen. 2010. "Lifetime Prevalence of Mental Disorders in U.S. Adolescents: Results from the National Comorbidity Survey Replication–Adolescent Supplement (NCS-A)." *Journal of the American Academy of Child and Adolescent Psychiatry* 49:980–989.

Morry, M. M., M. Kito, and L. Ortiz. 2011. "The Attraction-Similarity Model and Dating Couples: Projection, Perceived Similarity, and Psychological Benefits." *Personal Relationships* 18:125–143.

Oliffe, J. L., P. M. Galdas, C. S. E. Han, and M. T. Kelly. 2012. "Faux Masculinities Among College Men Who Experience Depression." *Health* 17:75–92.

Oltmanns, T. F., and A. D. Powers. 2012. "Gender and Personality Disorders." In *The Oxford Handbook of Personality Disorders*, edited by T. A. Widiger. New York: Oxford University Press.

Oltmanns, T. F., M. M. Rodrigues, Y. Weinstein, and M. E. J. Gleason. 2014. "Prevalence of Personality Disorders at Midlife in a Community Sample: Disorders and Symptoms Reflected in Interview, Self, and Informant Reports." *Journal of Psychopathology and Behavioral Assessment* 36:177–188.

O'Neil, J. M. 2008. "Summarizing 25 Years of Research on Men's Gender Role Conflict Using the Gender Role Conflict Scale: New Research Paradigms and Clinical Implications." *The Counseling Psychologist* 36:358–445.

Oshima, K. 2009. "Mother's Trust in Her Partner and the Daughter's Mental Health." *Japanese Journal of Developmental Psychology* 20:351–361.

Papp, L. M. and N. L. Witt. 2010. "Romantic Partners' Individual Coping Strategies and Dyadic Coping: Implications for Relationship Functioning." *Journal of Family Psychology* 24:551–559.

Penley, J. A., J. Tomaka, and J. S. Wiebe. 2002. "The Association of Coping to Physical and Psychological Health Outcomes: A Meta-Analytic Review." *Journal of Behavioral Medicine* 25:551–603.

Pierce, K. A., and D. R. Kirkpatrick. 1992. "Do Men Lie on Fear Surveys?" *Behaviour Research and Therapy* 30:415–418.

Rabinowitz, F. E., and S. V. Cochran. 2008. "Men and Therapy: A Case of Masked Male Depression." *Clinical Case Studies* 7:575–591.

Reissman, C., A. Aron, and M. R. Bergen. 1993. "Shared Activities and Marital Satisfaction: Causal Direction and Self-Expansion Versus Boredom." *Journal of Social and Personal Relationships* 10:243–254.

Ronen, T, and M. Rosenbaum. 2010. "Developing Learned Resourcefulness in Adolescents to Help Them Reduce Their Aggressive Behavior: Preliminary Findings." *Research on Social Work Practice* 20:410–426.

Sapolsky, R. M. 2005. *Monkeyluv: And Other Essays on Our Lives as Animals*. New York: Scribner.

Schrijvers, D. L., J. Bollen, and B. G. C. Sabbe. 2012. "The Gender Paradox in Suicidal Behavior and Its Impact on the Suicidal Process." *Journal of Affective Disorders* 138:19–26.

Schröder-Abé, M., and A. Schütz. 2011. "Walking in Each Other's Shoes: Perspective Taking Mediates Effects of Emotional Intelligence on Relationship Quality." *European Journal of Personality* 25:155–169.

Schwartz, S. H. 2012. "An Overview of the Schwartz Theory of Basic Values." *Online Readings in Psychology and Culture* 2:1–20.

Seibert, A. 2010. *The Survivor Personality.* New York: Perigee.

Simard, V., E. Moss, and K. Pascuzzo. 2011. "Early Maladaptive Schemas and Child and Adult Attachment: A 15-Year Longitudinal Study." *Psychology and Psychotherapy: Theory, Research and Practice* 84:349–366.

Smirnov, M. S., and E. A. Kiyatkin. 2008. "Behavioral and Temperature Effects of Delta 9-Tetrahydrocannibinol in Human-Relevant Doses in Rats. *Brain Research* 1228:145–160.

Smith, H. 2013. *Men on Strike: Why Men Are Boycotting Marriage, Fatherhood, and the American Dream, and Why It Matters.* New York: Encounter Books.

Smith, S. T. 2011. *The User's Guide to the Human Mind: Why Our Brains Make Us Unhappy, Anxious, and Neurotic, and What We Can Do About It.* Oakland, CA: New Harbinger.

Smith, S. T. 2013. *The Woman's Guide to How Men Think: Love, Commitment, and the Male Mind.* Oakland, CA: New Harbinger.

Solowij N., and R. Battisti. 2008. "The Chronic Effects of Cannabis on Memory in Humans: A Review." *Current Drug Abuse Reviews* 1:81–98.

Sutin, A. R., A. Terracciano, Y. Milaneschi, Y. An, L. Ferrucci, and A. B. Zonderman. 2013. "The Trajectory of Depressive Symptoms Across the Adult Lifespan." *JAMA Psychiatry* 70:803–11.

Tamm, L., J. N. Epstein, K. M. Lisdahl, B. Molina, S. Tapert, S. P. Hinshaw, L. E. Arnold, K. Velanova, H. Abikoff, and J. M. Swanson. 2013. "Impact of ADHD and Cannabis Use on Executive Functioning in Young Adults." *Drug and Alcohol Dependence* 133:607–614.

Treadway, M. T., J. W. Buckholtz, R. L. Cowan, N. D. Woodward, R. Li, M. S. Ansari, R. M. Baldwin, A. N. Schwartzman, R. M. Kessler, and D. H. Zald. 2012. "Dopaminergic Mechanisms of Individual Differences in Human Effort–Based Decision Making." *The Journal of Neuroscience* 32:6170–6176.

Tsirigotis, K., W. Gruszczyński, and M. Tsirigotis-Maniecka. 2014. "Gender Differentiation in Indirect Self-Destructiveness and Suicide Attempt Methods (Gender, Indirect Self-Destructiveness, and Suicide Attempts)." *Psychiatry Quarterly* 85:197–209.

Urbaniak, G. C., and P. R. Kilmann. 2006. "Niceness and Dating Success: A Further Test of the Nice Guy Stereotype." *Sex Roles* 55:209–224.

van Beek, Y., D. J. Hessen, R. Hutteman, E. E. Verhulp, and M. van Leuven. 2012. "Age and Gender Differences in Depression Across Adolescence: Real or 'Bias'?" *Journal of Child Psychology and Psychiatry* 53:973–985.

Vandello, J. A., and J. K. Bosson. 2013. "Hard Won and Easily Lost: A Review and Synthesis of Theory and Research on Precarious Manhood." *Psychology of Men and Masculinity* 14:101–113.

Van Vugt, M., D. De Cremer, and D. P. Janssen. 2007. "Gender Differences in Cooperation and Competition: The Male Warrior Hypothesis." *Psychological Science* 18:19–23.

Vohs, K. D. 2013. "The Poor's Poor Mental Power." *Science* 341:969–970.

Zvolensky, M. J., P. Lewinsohn, A. Bernstein, N. B. Schmidt, J. D. Buckner, J. Seeley, and M. O. Bonn-Miller. 2008. "Prospective Associations Between Cannabis Use, Abuse, and Dependence and Panic Attacks and Disorder." *Journal of Psychiatric Research* 42:1017–1023.

Whether an aggressor is a seasoned predator or an irate individual, hostility is almost always preceded by warning signs—if we know what to look for. *Surviving Aggressive People* dissects the psychology of aggression and exposes the subtle cues of impending violence. Most importantly, it contains timeless methods for transforming a potential disaster into a peaceful victory.

"An experienced psychologist, Dr. Shawn Smith has provided a readable and, most important, practical guide to prevent and defuse violence, whether one encounters it at work, at home, or on the street. Dr. Smith offers compelling vignettes to demonstrate his points. Readers will readily identify with many of the characters and situations. I recommend this book not just to professionals but also to the lay reader as he or she will emerge from reading it with a new awareness and valuable skills."

— Stanton E. Samenow, PhD
author of *Inside the Criminal Mind*

About the Author

Shawn T. Smith is a clinical psychologist in Denver, Colorado. He is the author of *Surviving Aggressive People*, *The User's Guide to the Human Mind*, and *The Woman's Guide to How Men Think*. He also writes a blog at ironshrink.com. Shawn lives with his wife and daughter, and their dog.

CPSIA information can be obtained
at www.ICGtesting.com
Printed in the USA
BVHW071354070521
606557BV00003B/180

9 780990 686422